Contents

99817

Part II: Technology and Copyright in Libraries and Classrooms

Part III: Beyond Four Walls

Po)Pso\

Technology and Copyright Law

A Guidebook
for the Library,
Research,
and Teaching
Professions

*Includes
1999 Supplement*

Arlene Bielefield and Lawrence Cheeseman

Neal-Schuman Publishers, Inc.
New York   London

Published by Neal-Schuman Publishers, Inc.
100 Varick Street
New York, NY 10013

"This publication is designed to provide accurate and authoritative information in regard to the subject matter covered. It is sold
with the understanding that the publisher is not engaged in ren-
dering legal, accounting or other professional service. If legal advice or other expert assistance is required, the services of a competent professional person should be sought." *From a Declaration of
Principles adopted jointly by a Committee of the American Bar Association and a Committee of Publishers.*

Printed and bound in the United States of America

Library of Congress Cataloging-in-Publication Data

Bielefield, Arlene.
   Technology and copyright law : a guidebook for the library, research,
and teaching professions / by Arlene Bielefield and Lawrence
Cheeseman.
      p.   cm.—(Libraries and the law series)
   Includes bibliographical references and index.
   ISBN 1-55570-267-8
   1. Fair Use (Copyright)—United States. 2. Library legislation—
United States. 3. Information services—Law and legislation—United
States. I. Cheeseman, Lawrence. II. Title. III. Series. IV. Series:
Libraries & the law series.
KF3030.1.B533   1996
346.7304'82—dc21   96-48255

Appendixes

1999 Update

List of Tables

Preface

Copyright is one of the most vexing problems facing librarians and educators today. Over the last several years, we have presented workshops and classes on copyright law to diverse groups of librarians and educators. During the question-and-answer portions of these presentations, we became aware of a widespread need for a book on copyright law and technology specifically tailored to those in the library, research, and teaching professions. Hence, this book, *Technology and Copyright Law: A Guidebook for the Library, Research, and Teaching Professions*, was born.

In both our speaking engagements and in writing our earlier book, *Libraries & Copyright Law*, we have found that discussing the history, intended purpose, and basic structure of copyright law results in a better understanding of the uncertainties and complexities new technologies create within the existing copyright law. Librarians, scholars, and teachers can make informed decisions about using copyrighted materials in their work—and are better able to judge when to seek legal advice on specific situations—when they have this understanding. All too often actions are taken and professional advice is sought *after* a problem exists, rather than before when there is no danger of a lawsuit against a school or educator who cannot afford the tremendous expense even threatened litigation brings.

Given the reality that our society is ever more a litigious one, we feel it is necessary that librarians, researchers, and educators learn how to practice *defensive law*. Like defensive driving, this method is intended to prevent trouble, heartache, and expense resulting from accidents—in this case legal accidents—by learning to anticipate problems and take affirmative steps to avoid them altogether. Today, it is crucial to foresee and prevent copyright problems *before* they occur, because even winning a case is expensive and time-consuming; losing a case is usually disastrous.

Since each copyright situation is different, care must always be taken. One should never assume that an action—especially whether or not a particular use of copyrighted material falls under fair use—can or cannot be taken based on someone else's experience. To make taking proper care even more cumbersome for busy librarians, researchers, and scholars (who rarely have either easy access to legal counsel or the funds to pay for such consultation), the copyright law seems at times to be almost incomprehensible. The old law school admonition to "Look to the language of the law" does not always make copyright situations any clearer—especially when the applicable law was written two decades before some of today's technologies became available. In many cases, the application of copyright law to technological formats is simply ambiguous and no one, even a copyright attorney, can predict with absolute certainty how a particular section of the law will be applied to a new technology until it is tested in the courts.

For example, consider the first sale doctrine (which holds that a copyright owner's exclusive right to distribute a work extends only to the first sale of a particular copy). This is the doctrine that allows American libraries to lend and circulate books and videotapes without paying a fee to the copyright owner. While this doctrine's applicability to books and videos is unquestionable, the situation is much less clear when it comes to videos, CD-ROMs and computer software.

Cases which will clarify the application of copyright law to new technologies *will* emerge. It is our hope that these cases will not be brought against schools and libraries (or those who work in them). To this end, we have explained the existing law and its development in detail using as plain and uncomplicated language as possible. We have also included a glossary to define words and phrases which might be unclear or whose understanding is crucial to making good decisions. We have also (with a great deal of trepidation) speculated as to what future legislation and judicial decisions might bring in this arena.

To facilitate use, we have divided the book into four parts. The first, "Copyright Law: Past, Present, and Future" discusses what the existing law was intended to accomplish, how it developed, and where we think it is headed. Part II, "Technology and Copyright in Libraries and Classrooms," provides guidance for making those copyright decisions—including fair use, library and archival exemptions, and licensing agreements—which librarians, researchers, and teachers most commonly face in their day-to-day work. This part of the book includes a number of special features (e.g., the "Fair Use Checklist" on page 79) that we designed to help you make good decisions in a timely, efficient manner. Part III, "Beyond Four Walls," deals with the electronic classroom and international copyright agreements.

The final part of the book isn't a formal section *per se* but rather a compilation of materials intended for ready reference and frequent consultation. These materials include: a glossary defining important copyright terms and phrases we have gleaned from relevant federal statutes and reports; the mandated wording and specifications for all copyright warning notices required in libraries; a list of the exclusive rights of copyright holders; a list of the limitations on those rights that are most important to educators, researchers, and librarians; legislative materials on Section 108 (the special privileges afforded libraries and archives); and the text of the innocent infringement exception for library or nonprofit educational employees (including teachers, principals, and superintendents) and the association of research libraries statement of principles on intellectual property.

We have at all times tried to cover both what the law *says* and what it does *not* say relating to everyday activities in libraries and schools. We hope this will assist you in practicing defensive law and responding appropriately to legal problems so that you succeed in protecting both yourself and your school or library without relinquishing either your rights or those of your students or users.

—Arlene Bielefield, J.D., M.L.S.
—Lawrence Cheeseman, M.L.S.

Part I
Copyright Law: Past, Present, and Future

1
Technology and the History of Copyright Law

- *Was the invention of the printing press responsible for the passage of the world's first national copyright statute?*
- *What can we learn about the relationship between technology and copyright law from the world's first national copyright statute?*
- *How have authors' rights changed since the invention of the printing press?*
- *What role did the first publishers association play in the development of copyright law?*

The right of authors to their own creations has been recognized since ancient Rome.[1] This right extended only to the original manuscript, however. Prior to the enactment of the world's first national copyright statute in 1710, authors could not legally make and sell copies of their own works. At best, they could only market a manuscript for a one-time fee. Once the original manuscript was sold, an author was not legally entitled to receive royalties or other compensation for the number of copies sold. In addition, without the protection of the law, authors could not control how their published works were presented or sold,[2] or even receive acknowledgment as the creator of the work.

In contrast, today's authors enjoy the protection of copyright laws that are almost universally recognized.[3] In the United States today, for example, copyright is more than just the right to make copies and to publish. Under current U.S. law, copyright is a bundle of exclusive rights granted to an author. It includes not only the right to reproduce (copy) and publish but also the rights to adapt, to perform, and to display a work.[4] In addition to these rights, some authors also have moral rights preventing any intentional distortion, mutilation, or other modification that would prejudice their

3

reputation.[5] Moreover, works that can be copyrighted are not restricted to printed text; they include maps, charts, designs, engravings, etchings, photographs, paintings, statues, musical works, motion pictures, and computer software. In fact, today's copyright law protects any original work of authorship fixed in any tangible medium of expression.[6]

What events were responsible for this fundamental transformation of the law? What could have caused such a profound turnabout, reversing centuries of tradition? In this chapter we will explore the role technology played in the historical development of the world's first national copyright law and show the role the printing press had in this dramatic paradigm shift.

THE PRINTING PRESS

The world's first national copyright law was the Statute of Queen Anne[7] passed by the British parliament on April 4, 1710 and taking effect six days later. The statute was enacted 255 years after the invention of the printing press and 233 years after William Caxton printed the first book in England.

At first glance, it might appear that there can be little, if any, real connection between the two events since

- They are separated by more than two and one-half centuries.
- Other important historical events took place in that same time period, including several that were much closer in time and relationship to the actual passage of the statute.
- An information revolution was already in progress.[8] The printing press was actually only the means for speeding up a manual operation that was already a growing industry at the time—the making of multiple copies of an original work.[9]

A strong case can be made, however, that the printing press and the enactment of the statute are directly related. In fact, the 233 years between Caxton and the passage of the statute can be viewed as necessary for development of the legal concepts in the statute. Also, before the invention of the printing press there was little need for a copyright statute. There were few legal problems because of the small number of copies then available. The opportunity to make illegal copies was limited and it was easy to determine who had stolen or plagiarized a copy. Thus, the same laws that were applied to real and personal property easily served for manuscripts and copies, without any undesirable consequences to the community or to local economies.[10]

This principle is illustrated by the first case in history involving literary property. In 567 Saint Columba (521–597), an Irish monk, on a visit to a neighboring monastery, made an unauthorized copy of the abbot's Psalter. When the abbot found out, he demanded that Columba immediately return the copy. When Columba refused, the abbot sought the help of a local king, who ordered the return of Columba's copy to the abbot under the principle "To every cow her calf."[11] Authors had a legal right to prevent anyone from copying their original manuscript without their permission, but once the manuscript was legally purchased, the new owner could allow another person to copy the manuscript without any compensation to the author.

Monasteries

Control over the number and quality of copies was also easy to maintain without the intervention of law. During the early Middle Ages monasteries had a complex set of rules that governed what works could be copied, who could copy them and for whom they could be copied. Monks went about their work with exceptional religious fervor, painstakingly copying and illuminating their works. Copying a long text could take as long as a full year. Scriptoriums were holy ground,[12] and copying was a sacred task.

Rise of Guilds

By the fifteenth century, the copying of manuscripts was commercialized and professional copyists appeared. These lay copyists found work plentiful and formed guilds, similar in function and purpose to today's trade associations. These guilds, like the monasteries, policed their own members and maintained high professional standards.[13] In contrast to the scriptorium, however, the lay copyists worked faster—using scripts that were easier and quicker to write and making heavy use of abbreviations.[14] Hence, the number of books increased dramatically and their prices declined. Students in the newly emerging universities could now have their own copy of a textbook, although they probably only rented it.[15]

Authors

During the Middle Ages, however, authors had to find rewards that were not monetary for their writings. This situation was perhaps not difficult to accept because large profits were never really available anyway. Truly popular authors became celebrities who often found rich sponsors to support them. Occasionally a truly resourceful author could find ways around the law to garner monetary rewards (for example, Boccaccio [1313–1375] rented his manuscripts to copyists).[16]

Letters Patent

Johann Gutenberg's (1400–1468) invention of movable type, along with the wide availability of paper, made it possible to produce almost unlimited exact copies of any title. The information revolution which had begun before the invention of the printing press now had the means to achieve even wider success.

At first, early printers proceeded in much the same way as their predecessors, the professional copyists. The rights to copy manuscripts were acquired from owners of manuscripts, including monasteries, libraries, or private owners. New manuscripts continued to be purchased directly from authors. In the case of ancient or medieval works, early printers often needed to compare several copies to determine the authentic text because progressive mistakes were often made in the hand copying process.

The new printing industry was at first a leisurely profession. There were many patrons who engaged printers, as they had copyists, to add to their own personal libraries. Thanks to the church schools, universities, and libraries, literacy and interest in learning were on the rise. Moreover, there were no laws or regulations governing printers' activities.

As the industry grew, however, competition between booksellers became fierce and manuscripts became harder to acquire. To gain an edge, booksellers sought the support and patronage of the Crown. Fearful of the power of the press to encourage insurrection, the Crown responded by granting to its trusted favorites the sole right to print a specific title. In some cases these grants covered a whole class of books. The king's printer, for example, had the sole right to print the Acts of Parliament and all law books.[17] Time limits were often attached to these royal grants.

These grants, which came to be known as letters patent, bear similarities to today's intellectual property law. Today's patents and copyrights are granted to an inventor or author who then enjoys the exclusive right to their creation for a limited time. In *Basket* v. *University of Cambridge*, Lord Mansfield referred to a letters patent granted to Cambridge University by Henry VIII in 1534 as the "copyright of the Crown."[18]

There is another similarity. Letters patent were more than patronage. Only printers who had gained the Crown's complete trust received these exclusive grants. The Crown was assured by these grants that printers would remain loyal and would only print works that were not seditious or heretical. In exchange for an exclusive right, the Crown gained control over the press. Today's copyrights also grant an exclusive right to an author, but it is given today in exchange for the furthering of knowledge and the sciences.

Stationers Company

The first letters patent was granted to Richard Pynson in 1518. In 1556 Queen Mary chartered the Company of Stationers, one of the first trade associations of printers and publishers. The 38 years between the two events saw the gradual acceptance of the Crown's authority to control the printing and publishing industry in England. Following the formation of the Company of Stationers, occasional letters patents were issued by the Crown, but the company took over their function acting in accordance with their royal charter.

In accordance with the company's bylaws, only members of the Company of Stationers were permitted to operate printing presses in England. In exchange, company members guaranteed and certified that all works published by them passed the censors and contained no insurrectionary material. The bylaws of the company also required members to record the title of the book in the Company's "Register-Book" and to pay a fee for any book they printed. Those who did not pay this fee or who printed books registered and recorded by other members were subject to fines, confiscation, or even imprisonment. Unlike letters patents which expired after a fixed number of years, the rights to print under the Company of Stationers bylaws were granted in perpetuity in the same manner that land titles were recognized under English common law.[19] The right to a registered title could be transferred or bequeathed in a will like the right to any other form of property.

This system gave the Crown absolute control over publishing. As stated by a judge in 1769: "By the charter of Queen Mary, the Company of Stationers was made a kind of literary constable, to seize all books that were printed contrary to the statute."[20]

Star Chamber

Disputes arising under the company's bylaws were submitted to the Court of the Star Chamber, which received its name from the stars painted on the ceiling of its hearing room. Unlike the regular common law courts in England, the Star Chamber was a court of equity.[21]

In 1556 the Star Chamber issued a decree regulating the number of presses and their manner of operation. This decree was modified in 1566. In 1585 the court declared that every book had to be licensed

> ... nor shall anyone print any book, work, or copy against the form or meaning of any restraint contained in any statute or laws of this realm, or in any injunction made by Her Majesty or her Privy Council; or against the true intent and meaning of any letters patent, commissions, or prohibitions under the Great Seal; or contrary to any allowed ordinance set down for the good government of the Stationers Company.[22]

In 1637 the Star Chamber codified its various decrees on book publishing into 33 clauses.[23] In its preface the Star Chamber spoke against the "enormities and abuses of disorderly persons professing the art of printing and selling books."[24] The decree declared in part that

- All books and pamphlets to be published shall be entered in the Register-Book of the company.
- It is the duty of company members to certify that any books or pamphlets that they publish do not contain anything contrary to church doctrine or against the state.
- No one shall print or import any book or pamphlet that another member has the sole right to print, under penalty of forfeiture.
- Every book or other work published shall bear the name of the publisher and author.
- Anyone who forges the name of the company or publisher on a book shall be subject to imprisonment.
- No one who has not been an apprentice to a company member for at least seven years shall sell any books or publications.
- No press shall be established or closed down without notice first being given to the company.
- The company is authorized to seek out and seize any press operating outside the authority of the company.

The Star Chamber was abolished in 1641, for largely political reasons, by the Long Parliament. The Star Chamber court had supported the Crown rather than Parliament in religious matters. Because the court operated without a jury, placed less emphasis on formal rules of practice, and conducted expedited trials behind closed doors, the term Star Chamber has unfortunately come to mean a court proceeding that is unfair and arbitrary.[25]

Parliamentary Acts

All of the court of the Star Chamber's decrees, including those regulating printing, were thus repealed. The Parliament acted quickly to restore controls on printing through a series of orders and acts. The Parliamentary Ordinance of 1641 prohibited printing without the consent of the owner of the copies.

The Licensing Act of 1643 called itself an act for "redressing disorders in printing" and basically renewed the Star Chamber's decree. Like its predecessor, the act required the licensing of presses and registration of titles with the Company of Stationers. Penalties under this act included forfeiture of copies to the owner. A new requirement was introduced, however, that copies of a work be deposited at the King's Library and at each of the universities. The primary reason for the deposit was to prevent fraud. In case of infringement, the copy of record would be the one on deposit. In this way, the courts could always be assured of having an unaltered copy to which to refer. The deposit requirement survives today and has proven invaluable to national library collections.

The 1643 act attracted considerable protest. John Milton (1608–1674), the poet and author of *Paradise Lost*, wrote four pamphlets between 1643 and 1645 dealing with divorce and published them without complying with the act. His *Areopagitica* was written in 1644 to protest the legalized censorship inherent in government control of printing and publishing.

The Licensing Act of 1662 had the stated purpose of prohibiting printing any

> heretical, seditious, schismatical, or offensive books or pamphlets, wherein any doctrine or opinion shall be asserted or maintained which is contrary to the Christian faith, or the doctrine or discipline of the Church of England, or which shall, or may tend to be to the scandal of religion or the church, or the government or governors of the church, state, or commonwealth, or of any corporation or any particular person or persons whatsoever.[26]

The act also required deposit of a copy and a statement at the beginning of the book that it contained nothing

. . . contrary to the Christian faith, or the doctrine or discipline of the Church of England, or against the state and government of this realm, or contrary to good life or good manners, or otherwise, as the nature and subject of the work shall require.

The act was periodically renewed, but due to continued protest and arguments for freedom of the press, it was finally allowed to lapse in 1694.[27]

Without the licensing acts, the only recourse for members of the Company of Stationers was to the courts. The penalty of confiscation and forfeiture was no longer available to them. As one member pleading with Parliament put it:

. . . the liberty now set on foot of breaking through this ancient and reasonable usage is no way to be effectually restrained but by an Act of Parliament. For, by common law, a *bookseller* can recover no more cost that he can prove the truth, nay, perhaps the hundredth part of the damage he suffers; because a thousand counterfeit copies may be dispersed into as many different hands all over the kingdom, and he not be able to prove the sale of ten. Besides, the defendant is always a pauper, and so the plaintiff must lose his costs of suit. . . . Therefore the only remedy by the common law is to confine a beggar to the rules of King's bench or Fleet, and he will continue the evil practice with impunity. We therefore pray that confiscation of counterfeit copies be one of the penalties to inflicted on the offenders.[28]

Despite repeated pleadings from publishers, Parliament refused to renew the licensing acts but instead embarked on a complete revision of the laws regulating printing and publishing.

FIRST NATIONAL COPYRIGHT LAW

Prior to the passage of the world's first national copyright statute, authors had few rights to publish their own works. Unless authors were also members of the Company of Stationery they could not register—and therefore could not print—their work. A letters patent granted by the Crown was rare and available only to the most politically well-connected author. An author's only recourse was to sell a manuscript outright to a member of the company. This was the case when John Milton sold his manuscript of *Paradise Lost* in 1667 for a pittance.[29] As a result, even the authors of very famous works were put in a dire financial position.

It was against this background that in 1710 the famous Statute of Queen Anne was passed. This statute remains the foundation of copyright law in England and the United States today. The full title of the act was "A Bill for the Encouragement of Learning, by Vesting the Copies of Printed Books in the Authors or Purchasers of Such Copies, during the Times therein mentioned" and it took effect on April 10, 1710.

The act began with the following statement of purpose:

> Whereas Printers, Booksellers, and other Persons have of late frequently taken the Liberty of printing, reprinting, and publishing or causing to be printed, reprinted, and published books, and other Writings, without Consent of the Authors or Proprietors of such Books and writings, to their great Detriment, and too often to the Ruin of them and their Families: preventing therefore such Practices for the future, and for the Encouragement of learned men to compose and write useful Books, may it please Your Majesty, that it may be enacted. . . .

For the first time in history the rights of an author to publish were explicitly acknowledged. Authors were to have the sole right of printing for a set period of time:

- for existing works—21 years from the effective date of the act
- for works not yet printed—14 years, and an additional 14 years if the author was still alive at the end of the first term

Books could not be imported without the written consent of the author or owner of the printing rights. More significantly, the penalty for selling counterfeit copies was forfeiture and the then substantial fine of one "peny" per page.

The act also set forth several preconditions which had to be met before an infringement suit could be brought. The book had to be entered in the Register-Book of the Stationers Company, and the suit had to be brought within three months of the offense. The deposit requirement was once again introduced and the number of required copies increased to nine. The act also provided for a subtle form of price control. If the asking price of a book was too high, the queen's officers could direct that it be lowered.

RIGHTS OF AUTHORS

The issue of authors rights was not settled by the passage of the Statute of Queen Anne. When the first term granted in the act expired in 1731 (21 years from 1710, the effective date of the act), a battle resulted over the rights to copyright. Owners of titles in the

Register-Book of the Stationers Company claimed that they had a copyright in perpetuity—after all, they had purchased the "copyrights" believing that they would not be limited in duration. Others held that the copyrights had lapsed according to the Statute of Queen Anne.

Common Law Copyrights

The right of authors to their manuscripts had been recognized since Roman times and had come to be known as the common law copyright. Many thought its basis was in natural law and that it existed with or without a statute.[30] What effect did the Statute of Queen Ann have on this common law right? It took over 40 years for this question to be settled.

In 1769 the case of *Millar* v. *Taylor* was brought before the King's Bench.[31] The question presented was whether authors had a common law copyright that was unaffected by the passage of the Statute of Queen Anne. Lord Mansfield and two other judges ruled that authors did indeed have a common law copyright that existed in perpetuity.

The issue would not be settled finally, however, until 1774 in the case of *Donaldson* v. *Becket*.[32] There, five points were considered before the House of Lords, Britain's highest court.

1. Do authors have the sole right of first printing and publishing for sale, and can authors bring an action against anyone who publishes and sells their works without their permission? The majority of judges voted that authors do have these rights.
2. Do authors lose these rights once the work is published, and could anyone then reprint a work without the author's permission? The majority of judges voted no, ruling that authors retain their rights even after publication.
3. Does the statute extinguish all of an author's common law remedies, and leave only those rights that are specified in the statute? By a one vote plurality the judges voted that authors' remedies are only those provided under the statute.
4. Do authors have the sole right of printing and publishing in perpetuity under common law? The court decided that authors have that sole right.
5. Is this common law right in any way taken away by the statute? Six to five the judges decided that the right is taken away by the statute.

In short, the judges ruled that authors do have common law rights, but these rights are taken away by the statute. After this case it was settled law in England that an author's rights can only be asserted by statute.

TECHNOLOGY AND COPYRIGHT LAW

There were 233 years separating the printing of the first book in England from the passage of the world's first national copyright statute. It took this long

- to experience the real impact of the invention of the printing press
- to develop the new legal concepts necessary to deal with that impact of technology
- for Parliament (the legislature) to become aware of the importance of this technology for the national economy
- to bring all of the parties together—the Crown, the Parliament, the Stationers' Company (the publishing industry), authors, and public support.

The following chronology shows the progress toward the world's first national copyright statute brought about by the invention of printing.

TABLE 1   Events Leading to Passage of the World's First National Copyright Statute

1477

Caxton prints *Dictes and Sayengis of the Philosophers*, the first book in England.

1504

First royal printer is appointed by the Crown. Various printers had cultivated the favor of the Crown to advance their own printing ventures. The Crown came to see the value in controlling the new print industry to help prevent insurrection.

1518

First letters patent is granted to Richard Pynson.

1530

Crown declares that printing is at its prerogative.[33]

1534

Letters patent granted to Cambridge University by Henry VIII.

1556

Queen Mary charters the Company of Stationers. The company was one of the major influences on development of the legal concepts inherent in the Statute of Queen Anne.

1585

Court of the Star Chamber decrees that every book printed in England is to be licensed.

1637

Court of the Star Chamber issues a comprehensive decree on book publishing. This decree forms the basis for all subsequent licensing acts passed by the Parliament and has a significant impact on the Statute of Queen Anne.

1641

Court of the Star Chamber is abolished by the Long Parliament.

1643

A licensing act basically renews the Star Chamber's decree of 1637. The act requires deposit in the King's Library and at each of the universities.

1644

Milton's *Areopagitica* is written to protest censorship and control over printing. The issue of freedom of the press advocated by authors will eventually persuade Parliament not to renew the licensing acts.

1649

A licensing act is passed despite protest from authors such as Milton.

1662

The last licensing act is passed.

1694

The last renewal of the 1662 licensing act lapses. The arguments of political philosopher John Locke for a free press had an important influence.

1695

Parliament refuses to renew licensing acts and embarks on complete revision of the laws regulating printing.

1707

A petition from some members of the Stationers Company is sent to Parliament. The petition argues that securing the rights of authors advances the public good.

1710

The Statute of Queen Anne, the world's first national copyright statute, takes effect on April 10, 1710.

ENDNOTES

1. See, for example, Richard Rogers Bowker, *Copyright: Its History and Its Law* (New York: Houghton Mifflin, 1912), 8.
2. Augustine Birrell in his *Seven Lectures on the Law and History of Copyright in Books* (New York: G.P. Putnam's Sons, 1899), 49, tells the story of how Erasmus found a novel way of getting back at a publisher, Frobenius of Basle, who published an edition of Erasmus's *Adagia* without seeking Erasmus's permission. Erasmus just moved into the publisher's house and continued to live there for some time rent free.
3. See Chapter 10 for discussion of the international aspects of copyright.
4. On November 1, 1995, the right of performing a sound recording publicly by means of a digital audio transmission was added. 17 U.S.C. §106.
5. Under Article 6bis of the Berne Convention, authors have the rights of paternity and integrity; that is, the right to be named as the author of the work and to object to any distortions or alterations of their work. In the United States, see the Visual Artists' Rights Act of 1990, P.L. 101-650, 104 Stat. 5128, 5133 (December 1, 1990).
6. 17 U.S.C. §102.
7. 8 Anne c.19. Sometimes called the Statute of Anne or the Statute of 8 Anne.
8. See Jay Tolson, "The First Information Revolution," *Civilization: The Magazine of the Library of Congress* 3 (January–February 1996): 52.
9. Birrell, 48.
10. Birrell, 41–42.
11. George H. Putnam, *Books and Their Makers During the Middle Ages: A Study of the Conditions of the Production and Distribution of Literature from the Fall of the Roman Empire to the Close of the Seventeenth Century* (New York: Hillary House, 1962), Vol. 2, 484–485.
12. See Putnam, vol. 1, 61 for the actual benediction used to consecrate a new scriptorium.
13. Morris Bishop, *The Middle Ages* (Boston, Mass.: Houghton Mifflin, 1968), 258–259.
14. Ibid., 259.
15. Ibid.
16. Ibid.
17. Birrell, 55.
18. 1 W. Blackstone, 121 (1758).
19. Putnam, vol. 2, 469.
20. *Millar* v. *Taylor*, 4 Burr. 2303 at 2374 (1769).
21. Courts of equity place less emphasis on formal rules of procedure, operate without a jury, and can grant remedies unavailable in other courts.
22. 28 Eliz. 4.

23. The list is recited in Birrell, 60–63.
24. Henry Hallam, *Constitutional History of England*. (New York: Sheldon & Co., 1862), 239.
25. The 1983 movie "The Star Chamber," about a group of vigilante judges who set up their own court and arranged the murder of criminals set free by the courts, capitalized on this interpretation.
26. 13 & 14 Car. II, ch. 33.
27. 1 Jac. 2, c.7, and 4 William and Mary, c.24.
28. 4 Barrow's 2317.
29. Birrell, 73–74.
30. Roman law was based on Stoic philosophy's view of nature, that a rational order existed before and despite manmade laws.
31. 4 Burr 2303.
32. 4 Burr 2408.
33. 25 Henry VIII, c.15.

2
Technology and Copyright Legislation

- *What was the source for the copyright clause of the U.S. Constitution?*
- *What happened to copyright formalities as new revisions of the law were passed?*
- *How has the definition of copyright changed?*

The first national copyright law, the Statute of Queen Anne, was never extended to the American colonies.[1] Yet U.S. copyright law clearly has its roots in it. Even though England and the United States were politically separated after the American Revolution, the statute still formed the basis of the U.S. Constitution's copyright clause and of the first copyright act in 1790.[2] In fact, even before there was a constitution, all but one of the original 13 states had passed their own copyright statutes based on the Statute of Queen Anne.

STATE COPYRIGHT LAWS

In May 1783, the Continental Congress recommended to the states that they pass their own copyright laws. Like the Statute of Queen Anne, the term of copyright under these state laws was 14 years with another 14-year extension. Some state statutes even contained a provision similar to the original English statute relating to price controls, which had been repealed in England in 1739. Ultimately, all of the states except Delaware adopted their own copyright laws.[3]

Even after a federal copyright law was passed, there would be two systems of copyright in the United States until 1978. Only published works received federal copyright protection; unpublished

19

works were protected by state law. Even today, works that are not in some tangible medium must look to state protection.

THE CONSTITUTION

The copyright clause of the Constitution and the Statute of Queen Anne share the same objective and means. The statute called itself "An Act for the Encouragement of Learning, by Vesting the Copies of Printed Books in the Authors . . . during the Times therein mentioned." The Act declared its objective to be "the Encouragement of learned men to compose and write useful Books. . . . " The statute achieves this by granting authors the "sole Right and Liberty of Printing" their books for the limited term of 14 years.

The copyright clause empowers Congress "To promote the progress of science and useful arts by securing for a limited time to authors and inventors the exclusive right to their respective writings and discoveries."[4] The objective of the clause is to "promote the progress of science and useful arts." It achieves this by "securing for a limited time . . . the exclusive right" of authors to their "respective writings." The copyright clause and the Statute of Queen Anne embody the concept, as expressed by the U.S. Supreme Court in 1954, "Sacrificial days devoted to such creative activities deserve rewards commensurate with the service rendered."[5]

The new American nation was so familiar with the events which led to and followed the statute's passage and with its provisions that the Statute of Queen Anne continued to serve as a model even after the two countries had separated politically. Moreover, Americans accepted the statute's underlying philosophy. It was unquestioned in America, as it also had been earlier in England, that the best means of advancing the arts and sciences was to secure authors' rights to their own creations. The copyright clause was part of the Constitution when it was adopted in 1787[6] and there was no evidence of disagreement among the drafters over its inclusion.[7]

Despite this common beginning, copyright law in the United States quickly evolved in its own direction, completely apart from England and, indeed, from much of the rest of the world. It would take almost 200 years for Congress to revise the copyright law to make it more compatible with most of the rest of the world. What finally led the United States to accept these changes? The answer to this question is at the heart of the relationship between technology and copyright legislation.

COPYRIGHT LAW REVISIONS

Copyright Law of 1790

As one of its first acts in 1790, the new U.S. Congress passed a national copyright law. This first U.S. copyright law, showing its roots in the Statute of Queen Anne, was entitled "An act for the encouragement of learning, by securing the copies of maps, charts, and books, to the authors and proprietors of such copies, during the time therein mentioned." The law granted authors who were citizens or residents copyright in books, maps, and charts for 14 years with renewal for 14 years more, if the author was living at expiration of the first term.[8] Procedures for acquiring a copyright were the following:

1. Before publication, a printed copy of the title of a map, chart, book or books was deposited in the clerk's office of the District Court where the author or proprietor resided.
2. The clerk of the court recorded the title.
3. Within two months, a copy of that record was to be published in one or more newspapers for a period of four weeks.
4. Within six months, a copy was to be deposited with the U.S. Secretary of State.

Failure to complete these procedures in the times specified and in the manner required resulted in loss of copyright.

The penalties for infringement were forfeiture and a fine of 50 cents for each sheet found. Half of the fine went to the U.S. government. The infringement suit had to be started within one year after the infringement occurred. The first U.S. copyright law made no provision for copyrighting works written by noncitizens or nonresidents of the United States, except to permit importation into the United States or reprinting or publishing in the United States.

Copyright Law of 1831

The first major revision of the copyright law occurred in 1831.[9] A major revision repeals all previous editions as well as effecting significant changes in a law.

Musical compositions, prints, and engravings were added to the list of items that could be copyrighted.[10] The first term of copyright was increased from 14 to 28 years. If the author, or his or her spouse or children were still alive at the end of the 28 years and still citizens or residents of the United States, the copyright could be renewed for 14 additional years. Thus, the maximum number of years that copyright protection could be continued under this act was 42.

Procedures for acquiring a copyright were the following:

1. Before publication, a printed copy of the title of book or books, map, chart, musical composition, print, cut, or engraving had to be deposited in the clerk's office of the district court of the district where the author or proprietor resided.
2. The clerk of the court had to record the title.
3. Within three months from publication, a copy of that work had to be delivered to the clerk of the district court.
4. At least once a year the clerk of the court had to send to the Secretary of State a certified list of all copies deposited.

For the first time, it was required that a copyright notice be printed in the work itself in order to secure a copyright. The notice had to appear on the title page or page immediately following if it was a book, or on the face or frontispiece of a map, chart, musical composition, print, cut, or engraving. The notice read: "Entered according to act of Congress, in the year ____ , by A. B., in the clerk's office of the district court of _____."[11]

Penalties for infringement included forfeiture and a fine of 50 cents for each sheet for books and one dollar per sheet for other works. In addition, the infringer was liable for all damages that resulted from the injury. Copyright owners could also obtain injunctions to prevent violation of their rights. All actions were required to be brought within two years of the infringement.

Copyright Law of 1870

The next major revision occurred in 1870. Paintings, drawings, chromos, statues, statuaries, and models or designs intended to be perfected as works of fine art were added to the list of items that could be copyrighted. Also added was the exclusive right to perform dramatic compositions publicly. In addition, authors could reserve the right to dramatize or translate their own works.[12]

Procedures for acquiring a copyright were:

1. Before publication a printed copy of the title of book or other article, or a description of the painting, drawing, chromo, statue, statuary, or model or design for a work of the fine arts had to be deposited in the mail, addressed to the Librarian of Congress.

2. Within ten days of publication, two complete printed copies of the "best edition" of a book or article (or a design or photograph in the case of a painting, drawing, statue, statuary, or model) had to be deposited in the mail, addressed to the Librarian of Congress. Books and articles for deposit could be sent postage-free.
3. No action for infringement could be brought unless a notice of copyright was inserted on the title page or the page immediately following in the case of a book, or on the face or front of other works.[13]

Publications previously sent to the Department of the Interior or to the clerks of the district courts were to be sent to the Librarian of Congress along with all records.

A penalty of $100 and forfeiture was provided for anyone who inserted a copyright notice and had not obtained a copyright. The penalty for infringing a copyright included forfeiture, fines, and damages.

Copyright Law of 1909

The next major revision of U.S. copyright law occurred in 1909. This revision remained in effect until 1978.

The total number of years that copyright protection was available increased to a total of 56 (§24 of the act). The manufacturing clause continued and expanded to require binding and typesetting as well as printing within the United States (§16).

Procedures for acquiring a copyright were:

1. Notice of copyright had to be affixed to each copy published or offered for sale in the United States (§10 of the act). The notice of copyright was generally indicated by "Copyright," "Copr.," or ©, followed by the name of the copyright owner and the year in which the copyright was secured (§17). Failure to include the notice resulted in loss of copyright forever.
2. Registration (§11) and deposit of two complete copies of the "best edition" with the Register of Copyrights (§13). No action for infringement could be maintained unless deposit and registration were complied with. Failure to deposit also could result in a fine and voiding of copyright (§14).

Copyright consisted of the exclusive right to

- print, reprint, publish, copy, and vend
- translate or make other versions
- deliver, read, or present in public for profit, if it be a lecture, sermon, address or similar production, or other nondramatic literary work

- perform or represent publicly a drama
- perform publicly for profit, if it be a musical composition[14]

Copyrighted works were classified into 13 categories for registration purposes:

- books, including composite and cyclopedic works, directories, gazetteers, and other compilations
- periodicals, including newspapers
- lectures, sermons, addresses (prepared for oral delivery)
- dramatic or dramatico-musical compositions
- musical compositions
- maps
- works of art, models or designs for works of art
- reproductions of a work of art
- drawings or plastic works of a scientific or technical character
- photographs
- prints and pictorial illustrations including prints or labels used for articles of merchandise
- motion-picture photoplays
- motion pictures other than photoplays.

Copyright also began with publication, creating a distinction between pre- and post-publication. After publication, the federal copyright provided protection. Prior to publication, authors had to depend on state law for protection. As in England, authors or their heirs had the sole right to an unpublished work in perpetuity (§2). Once published, it fell under the maximum federal protection of 56 years.

The Copyright Law of 1909 codified the "first sale doctrine" (§27). Under this doctrine, once a library has acquired a lawful copy, it may lend that particular copy, imposing whatever conditions it chooses. It can even resell that copy.

Copyright Law of 1976

The next major revision of the copyright law was passed in 1976 and became effective on January 1, 1978. This is the current copyright law in the United States, along with subsequent amendments.

The term of copyright protection was extended from the maximum length of 56 years to the more internationally recognized term of life of the author plus 50 years. For works made for hire, and anonymous and pseudonymous works the duration of copyright protection is 75 years from publication or 100 years from creation, whichever is shorter.

The act also eliminated the distinction between published and unpublished work—fixing copyright at the moment of creation rather than date of publication. The authors of unpublished manuscripts published after January 1, 1978, no longer retained their common law rights in perpetuity. Like other authors, their term of copyright became the same as that of published authors—life plus fifty years.

The act also did not make the failure to include a copyright notice on the verso (reverse side) of the title page a fatal mistake. Procedures to correct the omission were established. This was closer to the internationally accepted practice of recognizing copyright without a notice affixed.

In addition, the act expanded the types of works that could be copyrighted. Under the new law, copyright protects "original works of authorship" that are fixed in a tangible medium. "Fixation" means more than being directly perceptible. A work could be perceived through a machine or device. There are eight categories of copyrightable works:

- literary works
- musical works, including any accompanying words
- dramatic works, including any accompanying music
- pantomimes and choreographic works
- pictorial, graphic, and sculptural works
- motion pictures and other audiovisual works
- sound recordings
- architectural works

These categories are not viewed as exclusive. Computer programs, for example, are registrable as "literary works" and maps and architectural plans are registrable as "pictorial, graphic, and sculptural works."

The act incorporated the judicially created doctrine of fair use as part of the statute. Fair use allows copying of copyrighted works without the owner's permission for purposes such as "criticism, comment, news reporting, teaching (including multiple copies for classroom use), scholarship, or research. . . . "[15] Four factors are used to determine if a use is fair:

- the purpose and the character of the use, including whether such use is of a commercial nature or is for nonprofit educational purposes
- the nature of the copyrighted work
- the amount and substantiality of the portion used in relation to the copyrighted work as a whole
- the effect of the use upon the potential market for or value of the copyrighted work

Libraries and archives were given their own exclusive rights under Section 108 of the act. This section represented an outstanding victory for libraries.

In another section of the law, employees of nonprofit educational institutions, libraries, or archives who believed that photocopying done as part of their job was fair use would be treated as innocent infringers.[16] Their institutions would not be liable for statutory damages. They would, however, still be liable, if the photocopying was not fair use, to pay the actual damages done and profits lost.

INTERNATIONAL COPYRIGHT LAW

Each new revision of the copyright law

- added to the list of creative works that can be copyrighted (see Table 2)
- increased how long a copyright is in effect (see Table 3)
- made less cumbersome the procedures for acquiring a copyright (see Table 4)

As impressive as these reforms may seem, however, they did not keep pace with developments occurring in England and other countries' copyright laws.

Among the significant differences between U.S. copyright law and the copyright laws of other countries were

- Term of copyright protection. For example, in 1842 the term of copyright protection in England was already the life of the author plus 7 years. In that same year in America, it was only 28 years with a 14–year renewal.
- International copyright protection. For example, the U.S. copyright law did not offer protection to anyone but U.S. citizens and residents until 1891. An international copyright law had been passed in England in 1838. In 1885 most of the major nations of the world held a diplomatic conference resulting in the Berne Union for the Protection of Literary and Artistic Property (Berne Convention). Signers agreed they would recognize each other's copyrights and would make essential changes to bring their copyright law up to a high international standard. This became effective in 1887, but the United States was not a signatory to this convention because it could not meet the convention's standards.
- Manufacturing clause. Another major difference between U.S. copyright law and that of other major countries was the United States's long retention of the "manufacturing clause." The clause, which ac-

tually originated in England in 1534, made obtaining a U.S. copyright contingent upon printing in the United States. This clause survived through extensions until 1986 and because of it the notice printed on the verso of a title page states under the copyright notice "Printed in the United States."

The purpose of the 1976 revision of the copyright law was to bring the United States more in line with the copyright laws of other countries and to make it eventually possible for the United States to join the Berne Convention, the world's principal international copyright convention. Before this could be accomplished, however, several additional amendments to the 1976 revision were still necessary.

Computer software

In 1980, an important addition was made to the list of exceptions to a copyright owner's exclusive rights. The legislative history of the copyright act of 1976 includes the following statement in the House Report:

> As the program for general revision of the copyright law has evolved, it has become increasingly apparent that in one major area the problems are not sufficiently developed for a definitive legislative solution. This is the area of computer uses of copyrighted works: the use of a work "in conjunction with automatic systems capable of storing, processing, retrieving, or transferring information. . . . "[17]

Clearly Congress recognized that computer programs posed special problems. To contend with any anticipated problems that might arise, Section 117, "Scope of exclusive rights: Use in conjunction with computers and similar information systems," became part of the 1976 law.

In 1980, Congress changed both the title and wording of the section to its present format. Retitled "Limitation on exclusive rights: computer programs,"[18] Section 117 now allows the owner of a computer program to make another copy or adaptation of that computer program when

1. such a new copy or adaptation is created as an essential step in the utilization of the computer program in conjunction with a machine and that it is used in no other manner, or when
2. such a new copy or adaptation is for archival purposes only and provided that all archival copies are destroyed if the computer program is no longer rightfully possessed.

Under this section, placing a copy of a software program on a computer hard drive is permitted if it is essential to utilization of the program. The initially purchased disk or disks, then, would take on the status of archival copies.

Making archival copies is permitted for the purpose of backup, in case an original (or the copy on the hard drive) doesn't work. Multiple archival copies are not permitted—only one is to be in existence at a time.

In addition, Section 117 states that "Any exact copies . . . may be leased, sold, or otherwise transferred, along with the copy from which such copies were prepared, only as part of the lease, sale, or other transfer of all rights in the program."

Adaptations, on the other hand, may only be transferred with the permission of the copyright owner.

Phonorecords and computer software rentals

Phonorecords were eliminated from the first sale doctrine in 1984[19] and computer software in 1990.[20] Under these changes, particular copies of phonorecords and computer programs (including any tapes and disks) cannot be rented, leased, or lent either for direct or indirect commercial gain. Lending by nonprofit libraries and educational institutions, however, is permitted. A warning of copyright must be affixed to the package containing the computer program (see Appendix A). Anyone who distributes a phonorecord or a copy of a computer program in violation of these acts is an infringer, subject to criminal penalties. No later than December 1, 1993, the Register of Copyrights, after consultation with representatives of copyright owners and librarians, was mandated to submit to Congress a report stating whether the act had achieved its intended purpose while allowing nonprofit libraries to fulfill their functions.[21]

Berne Implementation Act

In 1988, Congress made the significant changes needed for the United States to sign the Berne Convention. Several of these changes had direct impact on libraries and schools. One of the most significant effects was the elimination of the copyright notice as a requirement for copyright. This means that a work created after March 1, 1989, may not have a copyright notice but may still be copyrighted. Also, deposit in the Library of Congress no longer affects the copyright status of a work, although deposit is still mandatory, and failure to deposit is still subject to fine. Registration of a copyrighted work is necessary only for bringing an infringement suit. As a result of the 1988 Act, the United States became a member of the Berne Convention on March 1, 1989.

Moral Rights

In 1990 Congress passed the Visual Artists Rights Act of 1990.[22] This act eliminates one of the principal obstacles to membership in the Berne Convention. It protects original works in single copies and limited editions, by preventing any intentional distortion, mutilation, or other modification of the work that would prejudice an author's reputation. The act also prevents any intentional or gross negligence that would result in destruction of a work of recognized stature.

Uruguay Round Agreements Act

As part of the General Agreement on Tariffs and Trades (GATT), the Uruguay Round Agreements Act was concluded on December 15, 1993. Over 100 countries, including the United States, agreed to significant reductions in worldwide trade barriers. Title 5 of the act includes an agreement on the Trade-Related Aspects of Intellectual Property (TRIPS).[23] Among the TRIPS provisions are the elimination of the sunset provision of the computer software rental act, a digital performance right in sound recording (antibootlegging),[24] and the restoration of copyright protection to works already in the public domain but still under protection in a GATT-member country that is the source of the work.[25]

Digital Performance Right in Sound Recordings Act

In 1995 Congress granted public performance rights to copyright owners of sound recordings. Sound recordings had been given copyright protection for the first time in 1971. Since Congress only intended that protection to prevent pirating of records, the full bundle of exclusive rights was not granted to sound recording copyright owners. "Specifically, they were granted only reproduction, distribution, and adaptation rights; they were not granted right of public performance. . . . "[26]

Why did Congress change its mind? CDs, a digital technology, had grown in popularity, quickly replacing phonograph records and analog tapes. It was also clear to Congress that the emerging digital transmission technologies offered new services that needed copyright protection if a new, vital industry was to develop. TRIPS also required member countries to have such antibootlegging provisions in their copyright laws.

Anticounterfeiting Consumer Protection Act

In 1996 Congress passed an act that specifically attempts to counter the problem of counterfeiting including copyright.

> It is estimated that businesses in the United States lose more than $200 billion a year today because of illegal counterfeiting compared to $5.5 billion of losses in 1982.[27]

Counterfeit goods also endanger American workers. Counterfeits have often gone undiscovered until they result in serious illness or injury.

PROPOSED LEGISLATION

National Information Infrastructure

In September 1995 identical bills were introduced in the House and Senate intended to adapt copyright law to the digital, net-worked environment of the future. S.B. 1284 and H.R. 2441 would add "transmission" to the exclusive distribution rights of a copy-right owner. Supporters of the bills contend that this is not a new right, but merely clarifies that the distribution rights of a copy-right owner can be exercised by transmitting a copyrighted work electronically.[28] In addition, the bills would expand the special ex-emptions for libraries and archives in Section 108 to permit digital copying and make other changes:

- under subsection (a) to reproduce *three* copies.
- under subsections (b) and (c) to make digital copies for the purpose of preservation, security, and replacement
- Libraries or archives would only be required to affix a copyright no-tice to a photocopy when the original work actually had a copyright notice.

This legislation did not pass. We encourage you to monitor copy-right legislation closely.

THE EFFECT OF TECHNOLOGY ON LEGISLATION

With the separation of the American colonies from England, the United States chose to go its own way from the rest of the world on copyright law. For almost 200 years the United States was not a signatory to the principal international copyright convention. The 1976 revision of the copyright law and several subsequent amendments made it possible for the United States to join the Berne Convention. Most recently the United States has signed the GATT agreement requiring even more changes to U.S. copyright law.

   While it is true that technology has been behind all revisions of U.S. copyright law, there is an even more significant force driving the changes—the growing importance of copyrighted materials to the national economy, particularly the U.S. balance of trade. U.S. copyrighted materials including movies and software are popular throughout the world. As a category, copyrighted materials represent a net gain to the U.S. balance of trade with the rest of the world.

TABLE 2   What Can Be Copyrighted

As the copyright law was amended, more and more items were
added to the list of items that could be copyrighted.

1790
books, maps, and charts

1802
designs, engravings, and etchings added

1831
musical compositions added

1856
right of performance of dramatic works added

1865
photographs and negatives added

1870
paintings, statues, and other fine arts added; right to translate or dramatize now belong to author

1909
rights of performance now include jukeboxes

1912
motion pictures added

1952
public performances for profit, recording of nondramatic literary works added to author's rights

1976
copyright law amended to cover original works of authorship
fixed in any tangible medium of expression, now known or later
developed, from which they can be perceived, reproduced, or
otherwise communicated, either directly or with the aid of a
machine or device (exceptions include works of industrial design and typefaces).

TABLE 3   Duration of Copyright

As the copyright law was amended, the number of years that copyright protection was available increased. After expiration of a copyright, a work enters the public domain and can be freely copied.

1790   14 years with renewal for 14 years more (total 28 years)

1831   28 years with 14-year renewal (total 42 years)

1909   28 years with 28-year renewal (total 56 years)

1976   life of the author plus 50 years (for joint works, life of the surviving author plus 50 years; for anonymous works, pseudonymous works, and works for hire 75 years from year of first publication, or a term of 100 years from the year of its creation, whichever expires first)

TABLE 4 Copyright Procedures

As the copyright law was amended, procedures for obtaining a copyright became less restrictive and formal.

1790
- deposit before publication in clerk's office of U.S. District Court
- notice published in newspaper four times within two months of publication
- copy deposited with Secretary of State within six months after publication
- no protection for imported works not written by a U.S. citizen
- penalties: forfeiture
- fines: 50 cents for each sheet found

1802
- copyright notice on or next to title page

1831
- copyright notice required in each copy
- newspaper notice no longer required except for renewals
- deposit with district clerk (transmittal to Secretary of State) within three months after publication

1834
- record of transfer or assignment of copyright in the court of original entry

1846
- delivery of copies to Smithsonian Institute and Library of Congress

1859
- repeal of 1846 deposit requirements
- Interior Department made copyright custodian

1865
- deposit with Library of Congress within one month of publication

1867
- $25 penalty for failure to deposit

1870
- prepublication notice required
- deposit of two copies with Library of Congress within ten days of publication
- print titles must be filed before publication

1874
- short form of copyright notice ("Copyright, 18__ , by A. B.") made legal

1891
- copyright extended to citizens of other nations if their country reciprocated and copyrighted item was printed in the U.S.

1893
- copies deposited "on or before publication" have the same legal effect

1895
- no U.S. government publication should be copyrighted
- penalties for infringement of photographs and of original works of art

1897
- unauthorized, willful and for-profit representation of any dramatic or musical composition is a misdemeanor punishable by imprisonment
- appointment of a Register of Copyrights in Library of Congress
- penalty for printing false claim of copyright
- importation of articles bearing false claim of copyright are prohibited

1900
- U.S. copyright law extended to Hawaii

1909
- copyright is effective by publication with statutory notice of copyright and deposit of two copies in Library of Congress
- manufacturing clause is extended to include typesetting, printing, and binding within the United States
- first sale doctrine

1955
- recognized Universal Copyright Convention

1956
- photographs of large, cumbersome works accepted in lieu of actual deposit

1976
- omission of copyright notice no longer results in immediate forfeiture
- single national system for both published and unpublished works
- manufacturing clause terminated

1988

- protection available to works distributed without copyright notice
- deposit and registration requirement still necessary for infringement suit

TABLE 5   What Is a Copyright?

The answer to this question depends on when it was asked.

1790

"sole right and liberty of printing, reprinting, publishing and vending such map, chart, book or books, for the . . . term of fourteen years from the time of recording the title thereof in the clerk's office. . . . " Chapter XV, 1 Stat.124 (May 31, 1790)

1831

"sole right and liberty of printing, reprinting, publishing, and vending such book or books, map, chart, musical composition, print, cut, or engraving, in whole or in part, for the term of twenty-eight years from the time of recording the title thereof, in the manner hereinafter directed." Chapter XVI, 4 Stat.436 (February 3, 1831)

1870

" . . . the sole liberty of printing, reprinting, publishing, completing, copying, executing, finishing, and vending the same [i.e., any book, map, chart, dramatic, or musical composition, engraving, cut, print or photograph or negative thereof, of a painting, drawing, chromo, statue, statuary, and of models or designs intended to be perfected as works of fine arts]; and in the case of a dramatic composition, of publicly performing or representing it, or causing it to be performed or represented by others; and authors may reserve the right to dramatize or translate their own works." 16 Stat.198 §86 (July 8, 1870)

1909

. . . the exclusive right:

(a) To print, reprint, publish, copy, and vend the copyrighted work;

(b) To translate the copyrighted work into other languages or dialects, or make any other version thereof, if it be a literary work; to dramatize it if it be a nondramatic work; to convert it into a novel or other nondramatic work if it be a drama; to arrange or adapt it if it be a musical work; to complete, execute, and finish it if it be a model or design for a work of art;

(c) To deliver, authorize the delivery of, read, or present the copyrighted work in public for profit if it be a lecture, sermon, address or similar production, or other nondramatic literary work; to make or procure the making of any transcription or record thereof by or from which, in whole or in part, it may in any manner or by any method be exhibited, delivered, presented, produced, or reproduced; and to play or perform it in public for profit, and to exhibit, represent, produce, or reproduce it in any manner or by any method whatsoever. . . .

(d)   To perform or represent the copyrighted work publicly if it be a drama or, if it be a dramatic work and not reproduced in copies for sale, to vend any manuscript or any record whatsoever thereof; to make or to procure the making of any transcription or record thereof by or from which, in whole or in part, it may in any manner or by any method be exhibited, performed, represented, produced, or reproduced; and to exhibit, perform, represent, produce, or reproduce it in any manner or by any method whatsoever; and

(e)   To perform the copyrighted work publicly for profit if it be a musical composition; and for the purpose of public performance for profit, and for the purposes set forth in subsection (a) hereof, to make any arrangement or setting of it or of the melody of it in any system of notation or any form or record in which the thought of an author may be recorded and from which it may be read or reproduced. . . . [29]

1978

Copyright protection subsists . . . in original works of authorship fixed in any tangible medium of expression, now known or later developed, from which they can be perceived, reproduced, or otherwise communicated, either directly or with the aid of a machine or device.[30]

Copyright in a work created on or after January 1, 1978, subsists from its creation and . . . endures for a term consisting of the life of the author and fifty years after the author's death.[31]

ENDNOTES

1. 8 Anne, c. 19.
2. Prior to the Constitution, all states except Delaware adopted their own copyright laws. Like the Statute of Queen Anne, the term of copyright protection was generally 14 years with another 14-year extension.
3. Massachusetts, for example, passed a copyright law in March 1783. The law was titled, "an act for the purpose of securing to authors, the exclusive right and benefit of publishing their literary productions for twenty-one years." The preamble to the Act stated in terms very similar to the Statute that:

   Whereas, the improvement of knowledge, the progress of civilization, the public weal of the community, and the advancement of human happiness greatly depend on the efforts of learned and ingenious persons, in the various arts and sciences; as the principal encouragement such persons can have, to make great and beneficial exertions of this nature, must exist in the legal security of the fruits of their study and industry . . . therefore, to encourage learned and ingenious persons to write useful books, for the benefit of mankind, be it enacted . . . .
4. U.S. Const, Art I, §8, cl. 8.
5. *Mazer* v. *Stein*, 347 U.S. 201 at 219.
6. Article I, Section 8, Clause 8 of the U.S. Constitution reads: To promote the progress of science and the useful arts, by securing for limited times to authors and inventors the exclusive right to their respective writings and discoveries.
7. In the *Federalist Papers* it was noted that this clause could "scarely be questioned" and the "public good fully coincides in both cases with the claims of the individual" (#43).
8. Copyright here means: "sole right and liberty of printing, reprinting, publishing and vending such map, chart, book or books, for the . . . term of fourteen years from the time of recording the title thereof in the clerk's office . . . Chapter 15, 1 Stat. 124 (May 31, 1790).
9. The act was entitled "An act to amend the several acts respecting copy rights."
10. Copyright under this act became: "sole right and liberty of printing, reprinting, publishing, and vending such book or books, map, chart, musical composition, print, cut, or engraving, in whole or in part, for the term of twenty-eight years from the time of recording the title thereof, in the manner hereinafter directed." Chapter 16, 4 Stat. 436 (February 3, 1831).
11. §5.
12. Under this act a copyright was: " . . . the sole liberty of printing, reprinting, publishing, completing, copying, executing, finishing, and vending the same [i.e., any book, map, chart, dramatic, or musical composition, engraving, cut, print or photograph or negative thereof,

of a painting, drawing, chromo, statue, statuary, and of models or designs intended to be perfected as works of fine arts]; and in the case of a dramatic composition, of publicly performing or representing it, or causing it to be performed or represented by others; and authors may reserve the right to dramatize or translate their own works." Section 86.

13. Under section 97, the copyright notice is to read: "Entered according to act of Congress, in the year _____, by A. B., in the office of the librarian of Congress, at Washington."

14. Chapter 320 §§1, 64, 35 Stat. 1075, 1088 (March 4, 1909).

15. 17 U.S.C. §107.

16. 17 U.S.C. §504 subsection c(2). Appendix E.

17. House Report (Judiciary Committee) No. 94–1476, September 3, 1976 (to accompany S.22, 116).

18. 17 U.S.C. §117, Pub. L. No. 96–517, §10(b), 94 Stat. 3028 (December 12, 1980).

19. "Record Rental Amendment of 1984", Pub. L. No. 98–450, 98 Stat. 1727 (October 4, 1984).

20. "Computer Software Rental Amendments Act of 1989", Pub. L. No. 101–650, 104 Stat. 5134, 5135, Title VIII, §§ 802, 803 (December 1, 1990).

21. This report, *Waiver of Moral Rights in Visual Artworks: Final Report of the Register of Copyrights*, was published by the Government Printing Office in March 1996. The Register concluded that no further legislative action is warranted.

22. Pub. L. No. 101–650, 104 Stat. 5128, 5133 (December 1, 1990).

23. Uruguay Round Agreements Act, Pub. L. No. 103–465 (October 18, 1994).

24. Digital Performance Right in Sound Recordings Act of 1995, Pub. L. No. 104–39, 109 Stat. 336.

25. GATT is treated in more detail in Chapter 10.

26. Senate Report (Judiciary Committee) No. 104–128, August 4, 1995 (to accompany S. 227), 10.

27. House Report (Judiciary Committee) No. 104–556, May 6, 1996 (to accompany H.R. 2511), 2.

28. Bruce A. Lehman, Assistant Secretary of Commerce and Commissioner of Patents and Trademarks, stated on November 15, 1995, before the House Committee on the Judiciary's Subcommittee on the Courts and Intellectual Property that "The proposed amendment does not create a new right. It is an express recognition that, as a result of technological developments, the distribution right can be exercised by means of transmission—just as the reproduction, public performance and public display rights may be."

29. 35 Stat. 1075 (March 4, 1909).

30. 90 Stat. 2544 (October 19, 1976).

31. 90 Stat. 2572 (October 19, 1976).

3
Technology and the Future of Copyright

- *What can we learn about the future of key copyright doctrines from their historical development?*
- *Why can facts and ideas be used even when they are part of a copyrighted work?*
- *Will the first sale doctrine remain relevant in the information age?*
- *Why is the relationship between the First Amendment and fair use important to educators, librarians, and researchers?*

Two hundred fifty-five years separate the invention of the printing press from the world's first national copyright statute. During those turbulent years the fundamental concepts of copyright law evolved. While many of the specific provisions of that first copyright statute have now disappeared, the key doctrines have survived, and continue to remain significant.

In this chapter we look at the impact of emerging technologies on the three key copyright doctrines most important to educators, librarians, and researchers. These doctrines are

- the first sale doctrine
- the concept that facts and ideas cannot be copyrighted even if they comprise a copyrighted work
- fair use

The first sale doctrine allows the resale or loan of a copy of a copyrighted work after it is first sold, without payment of an additional fee to the copyright holder. This doctrine is at the heart of such library activities as circulation. Without the first sale doctrine, friends of libraries groups could not hold fund-raising book sales. The doctrine that facts and ideas cannot be copyrighted and the doctrine of fair use allow the use of portions of copyrighted materials without first securing permission of the copyright owner or paying any licensing fee. The history and purpose of these doctrines will be used to determine if they will remain relevant. In addition, we will consider the relationship between the First Amendment and copyright, and how this affects the future of copyright law.

DEVELOPMENT OF COPYRIGHT LAW

The following changes that have occurred since the Statute of Queen Anne most affect educators, librarians, and researchers:

- It is no longer a requirement that a copyright notice be affixed to a work for it to be copyrighted. The © on the verso of a title page told educators, librarians, and researchers that a work was copyrighted and who owned the copyright. Today a copyright notice is only a recommended practice.
- Registration of copyright, which began in 1710 with the Register-Book of the Company of Stationers, is no longer required but *is* necessary to bring a copyright infringement suit in the United States.
- It takes considerably longer for a work to fall into the public domain. The original term of 14 years has now become the life of the author plus 50 years, or in the case of joint authors the life of the surviving author plus 50 years.[1] Legislation is pending that if passed will extend this term to life plus 70 years.
- It is only necessary to know when authors have died—not when their works were copyrighted. All works of an author enter the public domain in the same year.
- The types of items that can be copyrighted have been greatly expanded. The world's first copyright statute was limited to print materials.[2] Today's copyright covers any works fixed in any tangible medium of expression.
- The exclusive rights of copyright owners have been expanded. Under the Statute of Queen Anne, a copyright was the "sole Liberty of Printing and Reprinting."[3] Today copyright is a bundle of exclusive rights, including the right to reproduce, publish, adapt, perform, or display works.
- Copyright law has become a matter of international concern. International copyright treaties have brought dramatic changes to U.S. copyright law (see Chapter 10).

The basics of copyright, however, have not changed. A copyrighted work must still be an original work of authorship. More importantly, today's copyright statutes are still based upon the fundamental belief that the best way to encourage creativity is through the granting of an exclusive right for a limited period of time.

Since the first copyright statute in 1790, there have been major revisions in 1831, 1870, 1909, and 1976. Each of these revisions was due to developments in technology and the growing importance of these new media to the nation's economy. Congress took 65 years to craft the current revision of the U.S. copyright law. Broad, expansive language was specifically chosen to encourage the courts to apply copyrights to any medium "now known or later developed."[4]

It is certain, as it was in the past, that technological developments will continue to result in changes to copyright statutes. As in the past, these changes will not occur quickly. Legislators will wait to see how a technology develops and what effect it will have on the national economy. It is equally certain, as in the past, that the three key copyright doctrines will continue to evolve rather than perish.

FIRST SALE DOCTRINE

The first sale doctrine holds that a copyright owner's exclusive right to distribute extends only to the first sale of a copy.[5] Once a copy is lawfully acquired, the new owner is entitled, without the copyright owner's permission, to sell, lease, rent, give away, or otherwise dispose of that particular material copy.[6] The test used by the courts is whether the copyrighted object has been disposed of in such a way that the copyright owner has received the reward for its use.[7]

History

The first sale doctrine had its origins in the English common law relating to the sale of real and personal property.[8] The doctrine was first affirmed by the U.S. courts in the 1894 case of *Harrison v. Maynard, Merrill & Co.*[9] In this case, unbound leaves of books had been damaged by fire in a bindery. The bindery then sold the damaged leaves as waste paper. However, a second-hand book dealer later acquired the leaves, had them bound, and then began selling them as books.

The Second Circuit Court of Appeals ruled that the copyright owner could not prevent the sale of the bound leaves. While it was true that the second-hand book dealer could not legally print or publish an edition of the books, once the copies were sold the dealer was free to resell those particular copies without compensation to the copyright owner.

The first sale doctrine was later affirmed by the U.S. Supreme Court in the 1908 case of *Bobbs-Merrill, Co.* v. *Straus*.[10] Bobbs-Merrill, publisher and the copyright owner of a novel titled *The Castaway*, placed a notice in each copy just below the copyright notice stating that

> The price of this book at retail is one dollar net. No dealer is licensed to sell it at a less price, and a sale at less price will be treated as an infringement of the copyright.

To restrain R. H. Macy & Company from selling the novel at less than one dollar, Bobbs-Merrill Company brought suit. There was no contract or licensing agreement between the parties concerning the sale price. The Court held that while the copyright statute protects copyright owners' right to copy and sell their works, the law does not create the right to limit the price at which their works are sold by future purchasers who are not bound by contract or agreement.[11]

The first sale doctrine was first codified as section 27 of the 1909 copyright law.[12] It appears today as section 109 of the copyright law.[13] Congress has placed limitations on phonorecords[14] and computer programs.[15] Phonorecords and computer programs cannot be rented, leased, or lent for direct or indirect commercial gain. Any person doing so is an infringer, subject to criminal penalties.

The only exceptions are nonprofit libraries and educational institutions engaged in nonprofit lending. The current first sale doctrine holds that once such libraries or institutions have purchased (or have had purchased for them) any print media (such as books, periodicals, or pamphlets), phonorecord (LP records, audiotape, CDs, DATs, or any new media that may be invented), or piece of computer software (computer tape, disk, or other media), the library may lend that legally obtained copy without the permission of the copyright owner. For books and print matter, the library may lend the original as many times as needed. In addition, the library may make its own lending rules concerning the print material. There are some procedures that must be complied with concerning phonorecords and computer programs before they can be lent, including affixment of a copyright warning notice (see Appendix A).

Congress recently considered limiting the first sale doctrine for works of fine art and for exhibit photographs, but the final act[16] ended up only requiring a study of the problem.[17] The study was released in March 1996 and recommended that no further legislative action is necessary at this time. There have been no legislative attempts to repeal the first sale doctrine on books.

Purpose

As a congressional committee stated, "The first sale doctrine represents an important balancing of interests."[18] A purchaser should be able to dispose of a lawfully owned copy without obtaining a copyright owner's permission or paying any additional fees. At the same time, the exclusive rights of copyright owners, except distribution, are still preserved. The first sale doctrine was limited in the commercial renting of phonorecords and software because of compelling evidence that it would seriously damage two very significant industries.[19] Congress, however, made it clear that passage of these particular narrow limitations on the first sale doctrine were to have no precedential value.[20] In fact, during the same congressional session in which commercial record rentals were prohibited, a proposal to limit home taping of copyrighted materials for private, noncommercial use was rejected.[21]

Future

It is clear that if further limitations are placed on the first sale doctrine, a convincing case of actual or potential damage to an industry must be made.[22]

IDEAS AND FACTS

Copyright statutes in the United States up to and including the 1909 act spoke about the exclusive rights of authors in absolute terms. The 1790 act declared that copyright owners had the "*sole* right [emphasis added] and liberty of printing, reprinting, publishing and vending such map, chart, book or books. . . . "[23] The 1870 act added "completing, copying, executing, finishing"[24] to the list. The 1909 act, which remained in effect through 1977, further increased the list of "exclusive rights" and added only one limitation—the first sale doctrine. It was not until the 1976 act[25] that an enumeration of "various limitations, qualifications, or exemptions"[26] was actually part of the statute.

Despite this absolute language in the statutes, the courts developed doctrines on their own that would limit authors' exclusive rights. One of the earliest and most consistently held of these limitations has been the doctrine that facts and ideas cannot be copyrighted.[27] In 1991 the U.S. Supreme Court called this the "most fundamental axiom of copyright law."[28]

Even if a work is copyrighted, the facts and ideas that are a part of that work can still be used without the permission of the copyright owner. Only the author's particular expression of these facts and ideas is protected by copyright law. As the U.S. Supreme Court stated in 1991: "The mere fact that a work is copyrighted does not mean that every element of the work may be protected."[29]

History

The courts have found the basis for this exception in the copyright clause of the Constitution.

> To promote the progress of science and useful arts by securing for a limited time to *authors* and inventors the exclusive right to their respective *writings* [emphasis added] and discoveries.[30]

The clause uses the words "authors" and "writings." The courts have interpreted "authors" as meaning those who are the originators, makers, or creators, and "writings" as that which they originate.[31] "To qualify for copyright protection, therefore, a work must be original to the author."[32] It cannot be copied from another. Even when two works are almost identical, as long as each was independently created, both can be copyrighted.[33]

For a work to qualify as the writings of an author, therefore, the courts must determine that the work involved some kind of creative effort, no matter how modest that effort might be. Facts are not created; they are found.[34] Facts—including scientific, historical, biographical, and news—cannot therefore be copyrighted and must remain in the "public domain available to every person."[35] Facts existed before they were used in a copyrighted work and they would continue to exist even if they were not published in that work.[36]

While the underlying facts cannot be copyrighted, however, "the precise words used to present them"[37] cannot be copied without the copyright owner's permission. These words are original to their author. In 1985 the Supreme Court ruled that President Ford could not prevent others from copying the bare historical facts in his autobiography but he could prevent others from copying his "subjective descriptions and portraits of public figures."[38]

Purpose

The courts have also reasoned that granting a copyright to ideas would prevent others from using them and would thwart the copyright purpose statement of the Constitution, "to promote the progress of science and useful arts. . . . "

> The very object of publishing a book on science or the useful arts is to communicate to the world the useful knowledge it contains. But this object would be frustrated if the knowledge could not be used. . . . [39]

The idea limitation was incorporated in the 1976 act as section 102(b). In the House Report accompanying the bill it was made clear that this section "in no way enlarges or contracts the scope of copyright protection under the present law."[40]

Future

It is unlikely that Congress would limit this doctrine since it is based on the purpose statement of the copyright clause of the Constitution. To do so would almost surely limit the number of new works created and impede the progress of the arts and sciences.

FAIR USE

One of the important limitations on author's exclusive rights developed by the courts is the doctrine of fair use.[41]

History

The need for this doctrine was first expressed by Lord Ellenborough in an 1803 case: "while I shall think myself bound to secure every man in the enjoyment of his copyright, one must not put manacles upon science."[42] This same thought was expressed by Judge Leval who wrote in 1992 that the advancement of knowledge requires "some reasonable tolerance within which scholars and authors might freely use or quote from the writings of others for comment, criticism, debate, history, etc."[43]

The term "fair use" was actually first used in 1869,[44] but the doctrine received its classic formulation in 1841. Justice Story reasoned that to determine whether a use violates the copyright law:

> ... look to the nature and objects of the selection made, the quantity and value of the materials used and the degree in which the use may prejudice the sale or diminish the profits or supersede the objects of the original work.[45]

When the fair use doctrine was codified as section 107 of the 1976 copyright law (see Chapter 4),[46] Congress used Justice Story's formulation.[47]

Purpose

The courts and Congress have found the rationale behind the fair use doctrine in the purpose statement of the copyright clause of the Constitution. The constitutional purpose in granting copyright protection in the first place[48] is "To Promote the Progress of Science and Useful Arts." To serve that end, courts "must occasionally subordinate the copyright holder's interest in a maximum financial return to the greater public interest in the development of art, science and industry."[49]

In addition, as Justice Story explained,

> —[i]n truth, in literature, in science and in art, there are, and can be, few, if any, things, which in an abstract sense, are strictly new and original throughout. Every book in literature, science and art, borrows, and must necessarily borrow, and use much which was well known and used before.[50]

Future

Since the fair use doctrine has its basis in the purpose statement of the copyright clause of the Constitution, its function goes to the heart of copyright. The fair use doctrine was developed by the courts even without a statutory provision. When Congress added it to the 1976 act, they made it clear that the law "endorses the purpose and general scope of the judicial doctrine of fair use, but there is no disposition to freeze the doctrine in the statute, especially during a period of rapid technological change."[51]

As the rights of copyright owners have been expanded by Congress, the importance of the fair use exception has increased. Adaptations such as translations, abridgments, or condensations were once not part of the rights of a copyright owner and were considered new works, not requiring the original author's consent. In the 1976 act, Congress carefully included the first statutory recognition of fair use to balance the addition of adaptations to the bundle of exclusive rights of copyright owners.

Today questions are being raised about the vitality of fair use in an electronic environment. Will fair use be replaced by licensing agreements? It is unlikely. Educators, librarians, and researchers should not have to pay for copying that qualifies as fair use.

In addition, fair use is necessary to prevent copyright law from resulting in censorship and in violating the First Amendment. This need is best illustrated by a 1966 case involving the publication of a biography of Howard Hughes.[52] On May 26, 1966, Rosemont Enterprises, Inc., acting for Howard Hughes, brought a lawsuit in a U.S. District Court for the Southern District of New York alleging that its copyrights to a series of articles, which appeared in *Look* magazine in early 1954, were infringed by a biography that Random House planned to publish. It was clear to the court that Howard Hughes had purchased the rights to the *Look* articles solely to prevent publication of the biography since any biographer would have to rely very heavily on the *Look* articles. Despite this, the District Court issued an injunction.

On appeal, the U.S. Court of Appeals for the Second Circuit overruled and vacated the injunction. The Second Circuit based its reasoning completely on the fair use doctrine. The court noted that it is customary for biographers to refer to and quote earlier works. "This practice is permitted because of the public benefit in encouraging the development of historical and biographical works and their public distribution. . . . "[53]

The court noted that, of course, an author cannot avoid independent research by simply copying another's work and calling that fair use. "The fair use privilege is based on the concept of reasonableness and extensive verbatim copying or paraphrasing of material set down by another cannot satisfy that standard."[54]

Finally, the court pointed out that an injunction is a drastic remedy, particularly when dealing with a book.[55] The court needed a more compelling argument before intruding "into an area fraught with sensitivity in its possible impingement upon fundamental democratic and intellectual institutions. . . . "[56] If the fair use doctrine had not been available in this case, a permanent injunction would have definitely been issued. This case raises the larger issue of the relationship between the First Amendment and copyright.

FIRST AMENDMENT

The First Amendment to the Constitution reads in part: "Congress shall make no laws . . . abridging the freedom of speech. . . . "[57] This statement has come to be known as the speech clause. The copyright clause of the Constitution reads:

> To promote the progress of science and useful arts by securing for a limited time to authors and inventors the exclusive right to their respective writings and discoveries.[58]

At first glance it is hard to see how these two clauses are related, let alone conflicting.

History

The copyright clause of the Constitution was part of the U.S. Constitution when it was adopted in 1787. There is no evidence of any disagreement among the drafters of the Constitution over this clause. In the *Federalist Papers* it was noted that this clause could "scarcely be questioned."[59]

In contrast, the First Amendment was not part of the Constitution as it was originally drafted. In the closing days of the Constitutional Convention, several proposals to add a bill of rights were voted down with relatively little discussion. While the exact reasons are not known, many delegates may have felt that a national bill of rights was simply unnecessary because the new federal government did not have any powers that would require such prohibitions. Some delegates may have feared that a bill of rights would add to the controversy already surrounding the Constitution, just as it was being submitted to the states for ratification. Other delegates may have been mindful of the late hour.

After the Constitution was finally signed by the delegates on September 17, 1787, and submitted to the states for ratification, the lack of a bill of rights drew more public criticism than any other aspect of the Constitution. It thus became clear that the Constitution would not be ratified by the states without firm assurance from its drafters that a bill of rights would be approved in the form of amendments to the new Constitution at the very first session of Congress. The promise was made and the Constitution was ratified by the required nine states on June 21, 1788, with the understanding that the new Congress would draft and recommend to the states the adoption of such a bill of rights.

At the first session of Congress, a copyright law was passed and the promised amendments to the Congress were sent on to the states for ratification. On December 15, 1791, the amendments were ratified by 11 of the 14 states and added to the Constitution. Six months earlier on May 31, 1790, the new copyright law had been approved.[60]

Purpose

The purpose of the copyright clause is stated clearly within it. Copyrights are granted because they advance the public good of furthering knowledge and the arts. This is achieved by granting to copyright owners the exclusive rights to their works for a limited time. A young democracy needed to encourage the creative activities of its citizens in order to survive and to grow. The unprecedented growth in inventions, scientific discoveries, technological advances, and literary works can be directly attributed to America's copyright and patent laws.

On the other hand, the purpose of the speech clause is not contained within it. It is also unclear from the records of the Constitutional Convention or from the debate in the House what were the real purposes behind the speech clause. There is no record of any debate in the Senate or in the states during ratification. The lack of interest in debate is probably because the amendment was not seen as a novel principle of government but rather the continuation of rights guaranteed from their English ancestry.[61] Because of this, the courts have been required to identify the purposes behind the speech clause.

One of the most important and unquestioned[62] of these purposes is to insure "unfettered interchange of ideas for the bringing about of political and social changes desired by the people."[63] Before coming to America the colonists had seen firsthand the abuses of sovereign governments in Europe. In fact, many of the colonists had come to America to escape the religious and political persecutions of such governments. Prior to the Revolution, the British government also resorted to repressive means to prevent the loss of its American colonies. Severe restrictions were placed on freedom of religion, press, assembly, and speech in an unsuccessful attempt to suppress the insurrection. These experiences convinced the colonists that there had to be a new, different kind of government.

It is this revolutionary change in the role of government that is primarily responsible for Americans' unprecedented access to government and all other types of information. Under the British, the Crown was sovereign and the people were subjects. Under the Constitution, it is the people, not the government, that possess absolute sovereignty. The power to censor must be exercised by the people over government, not by the government over people. Government could no longer limit access to information without a compelling and significant reason.

In addition, this revolution required an educated populace—citizens who were informed and capable of governing themselves. To make the best decisions, there must be vigorous debate in order to find the best solutions to the problems facing the young country. As the colonists had learned, truth is more likely to be gathered out of a multitude of tongues than through any kind of authoritative pronouncement. As Justice Holmes stated in a 1919 U.S. Supreme Court decision: the "best test of truth is the power of the thought to get itself accepted in the competition of the market. . . . "[64] It is for this reason that debate on public issues should be uninhibited, robust, and wide-open, and may well include vehement, caustic, and sometimes unpleasant attacks.[65]

There are obvious risks to government in encouraging such "unfettered interchange of ideas"[66] but the experiences of the colonists convinced them that it was far more hazardous to discourage thought. Only such open public debate could bring about desirable political and social changes in a lawful manner.[67] The safest path was not through repression but through the opportunity to discuss grievances and remedies freely.[68]

Under such a government the state must make it possible for its citizens to develop their reading and reasoning skills fully. Citizens must have access to new, different, and challenging thoughts and ideas. "The greatest menace to freedom is an inert people. . . . "[69] In a 1927 concurring opinion, Justices Brandeis and Holmes gave this view a classic formulation that deserves to be quoted in full:

> Those who won our independence believed that the final end of the State was to make men free to develop their faculties; and that in its government the deliberative forces should prevail over the arbitrary. They believed that freedom to think as you will and to speak as you think are means indispensable to the discovery and spread of political truth; that without free speech and assembly discussion would be futile; that with them, discussion affords ordinarily adequate protection against the dissemination of noxious doctrine; that the greatest menace to freedom is an inert people. . . . [70]

That is, governments are established to encourage self-actualization (the freedom to develop your faculties), liberty (both as an end and a means), truth (freedom to think and to speak are indispensable to finding the truth), and freedom to change (inertia is the greatest enemy).

Conflict

It is clear that the drafters of the Constitution did not see any conflict between these two clauses since they were written at almost the same time. Moreover, the goal of both clauses was the same—to advance the public good by expanding knowledge.

If the prohibitions in the speech and copyright clauses are interpreted in the absolute sense in which they are written, however, a conflict arises. The speech clause states that Congress "shall not make" any laws inhibiting freedom of speech. The copyright clause refers to the "exclusive" right of an author. No one would be able to copy an author's expression without permission of the author. If both clauses are taken as they are written, speech would be inhibited whenever a copyrighted work was involved.

The drafters of the speech clause themselves recognized limitations on speech. Libel and obscenity were never seen as falling within the constitutionally protected area of speech. Obscenity was excluded because it had nothing to do with unfettered interchange of ideas for bringing about political or social change.[71] Obscenity did not play an essential part in the exposition of ideas and was of such slight social value that any benefit from it was outweighed by the social interest in order and morality.[72]

The courts have not interpreted or applied either the speech or copyright clause in the absolute terms in which they are written. Freedom of speech does not confer an absolute right to speak without responsibility. For one, it does not mean that anyone with an opinion or belief may address a group at any public place and at any time.[73] No one can ignore a red light as a means of social protest, and no one would defend a street meeting in the middle of Times Square at rush hour as a form of freedom of speech.

Congress has also not seen authors' rights to their publications as being absolutely "exclusive." In the current U.S. copyright law the exclusive rights of the owner of a copyright are set forth in section 106. Sections 107 through 120 then go on to set forth the limitations on those exclusive rights.[74] The courts have also acted to limit the rights of copyright owners. For example, copyright owners cannot claim ownership of facts or ideas contained within their works.[75]

If the clauses are not to be read in absolute terms, is it still possible for the clauses to conflict? How do the courts deal with copyright cases that involve First Amendment rights? Has the Supreme Court dealt with this issue?

The Supreme Court has not yet discussed this issue. Several lower federal courts have. In 1972 the U.S. District Court for the Northern District of California in *Walt Disney Productions* v. *Air Pirates*[76] dealt with a copyright infringement case that had First Amendment implications. The suit involved the use of Mickey Mouse in a literary criticism. The question raised in this case was whether the First Amendment affected copyright protection.

The court ruled that this use of Mickey Mouse amounted to a "substantial taking."[77] The First Amendment was not a defense because the message could have been conveyed without using a copyrighted cartoon character. Ideas can be expressed in innumerable ways without copying someone else's particular expressions. Anyone who wants to express his or her views about a mouse can do so without using Disney's Mickey Mouse.

In 1977 the U.S. Court of Appeals for the Ninth Circuit (California) considered the relationship between copyright and the First Amendment in the case of *Sid & Marty Krofft Television* v. *McDonald's Corporation*.[78] This case considered whether a television commercial promoting McDonald's restaurants infringed on a copyrighted television show *H. R. Pufnstuf*. McDonald's contended that the First Amendment limited copyright protection and that an infringement case involving First Amendment rights therefore required a more demanding standard.[79] The court relied heavily on the earlier Walt Disney case and ruled that no First Amendment considerations operate since alternative means of expression existed. The court did, however, conclude that under rare circumstances the First Amendment can limit copyright protection. The instance cited was the 1968 case of *Time, Inc.* v. *Bernard Geis Associates*[80] heard in the Southern District Court of New York. The case involved copying frames of the Zapruder film of the Kennedy assassination. The District Court did not directly mention the First Amendment but did hold that the right to copy the film was justified because of "public interest in having the fullest information available in the murder of President Kennedy."[81]

In 1982 another federal circuit court considered a First Amendment case involving a news event, the death of Charlie Chaplin. In *Roy Export Co. Estab. of Vaduz* v. *Columbia Broadcasting*[82] CBS argued that its right to report a newsworthy event shielded it from copyright liability and allowed it to use copyrighted clips from Chaplin films. The court found CBS' arguments unpersuasive. The court pointed out that circuit courts that had considered the relationship between the First Amendment and copyright reduced it to the fair use defense.

THE FUTURE OF KEY COPYRIGHT DOCTRINES

Many of the original provisions of the world's first copyright statute have disappeared, but the key doctrines have survived and continue to develop. It is also clear that these doctrines should continue to be adapted to emerging technologies.

The first sale doctrine is at the heart of library activities and has its roots deep in English common law. The key doctrines of fair use and the fact/idea limitation on an author's exclusive rights are both rooted in the copyright clause of the Constitution. In addition there would be a conflict between copyright and the First Amendment without these doctrines. One does not have to copy a copyrighted expression—the ideas and facts behind it can be conveyed without violating copyright law. In instances where the expression is fair use, one is free to use the expression without the owner's permission.

ENDNOTES

1. In European countries, including England, it is 70 years after the death of the author.
2. The first U.S. copyright statute in 1790 also included maps and charts.
3. 8 Anne c.19.
4. 17 U.S.C. §102.
5. *United States* v. *Gross*, 803 F.2d 638 at 643 (1986).
6. 17 U.S.C. § 109(a) states:
   Notwithstanding the provisions of section 106(3), the owner of a particular copy or phonorecord lawfully made under this title, or any person authorized by such owner, is entitled, without the authority of the copyright owner, to sell or otherwise dispose of the possession of that copy or phonorecord.
7. *United States* v. *Masonite Corp.*, 316 U.S. 265 at 278 (1942).
8. "The first sale doctrine has its roots in the English common law rule against restraints on alienation of property." House Report No. 98-987 (to accompany H.R. 98-987), 2.
9. 51 F. 689.
10. 210 U.S. 339.
11. Ibid. at 350.
12. 17 U.S.C. §27 (1909) states:

The copyright is distinct from the property in the material object copyrighted, and the sale or conveyance, by gift or otherwise, of the material object shall not of itself constitute a transfer of the title to the material object; but nothing in this title shall be deemed to forbid, prevent, or restrict the transfer of any copy of a copyrighted work the possession of which has been lawfully obtained.

13. Entitled *Limitations on exclusive rights: Effect of transfer of particular copy or phonorecord*, the section reads simply:

    (a) Notwithstanding the provisions of section 106(3), the owner of a particular copy or phonorecord lawfully made under this title, or any person authorized by such owner, is entitled, without the authority of the copyright owner, to sell or otherwise dispose of the possession of that copy or phonorecord.

14. Record Rental Act of 1984, P.L. No. 98-450.

15. Computer Software Rental Amendments Act of 1990, P.L. No. 101-650.

16. Visual Artists Right Act of 1990, P.L. No. 101-650.

17. The report was done by Marybeth Peters, Register of Copyrights and is entitled, *Waiver of Moral Rights in Visual Artworks: Final Report of the Register of Copyrights* (Library of Congress, U.S. Copyright Office). It is available from the Government Printing Office.

18. House Report (Judiciary Committee) No. 101-735, September 21, 1990 (to accompany H.R. 5498), 7.

19. House Report (Judiciary Committee) No. 98-987, August 31, 1984 (to accompany H.R. 5938), 2.

20. Ibid.

21. Ibid.

22. The *Final Report of the Working Group on Intellectual Property* contends that the first sale doctrine does not apply to electronic transmissions because a computer loads the original in temporary memory (RAM) and then copies and sends it out. The first sale doctrine does not include the right to make a copy.

23. Chapter XV, 1 Stat. 124 (May 31, 1790).

24. 16 Stat. 198 §86 (July 8, 1870).

25. 90 Stat. 2541 (October 19, 1976).

26. House Report No. 94-1476, 61–62.

27. *Baker* v. *Selden*, 101 U.S. 99 (1897).

28. *Feist Publication, Inc.* v. *Rural Telephone Service*, 499 U.S. 340 at 344.

29. Ibid., 348.

30. U.S. Const., Art I, §8, cl. 8.

31. *Burrow-Giles Lithographic Co.* v. *Savony*, 111 U.S. 53 at 58 (1884) observed that

    By writings in that clause is meant the literary productions of those authors, and Congress very properly has declared these to include all forms of writing, printing, engraving, etching, &c., by which the ideas in the mind of the author are given visible expression.

32. *Feist*, 345.

33. Ibid., 346.
34. "The first person to find and report a particular fact has not created the fact; he or she has merely discovered its existence." Ibid., 347.
35. *Miller* v. *Universal City Studios, Inc.*, 650 F.2d 1365 at 1369 (1981).
36. *Feist*, 361.
37. Ibid., 348.
38. *Harper & Row, Publishers, Inc.* v. *National Enterprises*, 471 U.S. 539 at 556–557.
39. *Baker*, 103.
40. House Report No. 94-1476 (Committee on the Judiciary), 14.
41. Notes of the Committee on the Judiciary, House Report No. 94-1476. "The judicial doctrine of fair use, one of the most important and well-established limitations on the exclusive right of copyright owners, would be given express statutory recognition for the first time in section 107."
42. *Carey* v. *Kearsley*, 4 Esp. 168 at 170.
43. *American Geophysical Union* v. *Texaco Inc.*, 802 F. Supp. 1 at 10.
44. *Lawrence* v. *Dana*, 15 F. Cas. 26 (C.C.D. Mass.).
45. 9 F. Cas. 342 at 348.
46. As stated in *Sony Corp. of America* v. *Universal Studios, Inc.*, 464 U.S. 417 at 447 n.29:
    The Copyright Act of 1909, 35 Stat. 1075, did not have a "fair use" provision. Although that Act's compendium of exclusive rights "to print, reprint, publish, copy, and vend the copyrighted work" was broad enough to encompass virtually all potential interactions with a copyrighted work, the statute was never so construed. The courts simply refused to read the statute literally in every situation. When Congress amended the statute in 1976, it indicated that it "intended to restate the present judicial doctrine of fair use, not to change, narrow, or enlarge it in any way." House Report No. 94-1476 (1976), 66.
47. The *first* factor, the purpose and character of the use, was drawn from "the objects of the selections made . . . and the degree to which the use . . . may supersede the objects of the original work." The *second* factor, the nature of the copyright work, from "nature . . . of the selections made . . . and the degree to which the use . . . may supersede the objects of the original work." The *third* factor, the amount and substantiality of the portion used, was drawn from "the quantity . . . of the materials used and the degree in which the use . . . may supersede the objects of the original work." The *fourth* factor, the effect on the use on the potential market for the copyright, from " degree in which the use may prejudice the sale or diminish the profits.
48. *Mathews Conveyor Co.* v. *Palmer-Bee Co.*, 135 F.2d 73 (1943).
49. *Berlin* v. *E.C. Publications Inc.*, 329 F.2d 541 at 544(1964).
50. *Emerson* v. *Davies*, 8 F. Cas. 615, 619 (No. 4,436) (CCD Mass. 1845).
51. House Report No. 94-1476, 74.
52. *Rosemont Enterprises, Inc.* v. *Random House, Inc.*, 366 F.2d 303 (1966).
53. Ibid., 307.

54. Ibid., 310.
55. Ibid., 311 quoting *In Pocket Books, Inc.* v. *Dell Publishing*, 49 Misc.2d 252 at 256 (1966).
56. Ibid. Citing *In Estate of Hemingway* v. *Random House*, 49 Misc.2d 726 at 728 (1966).
57. U.S. Const, Amend. I.
58. U.S. Const, Art I, §8, cl. 8.
59. #43.
60. Chapter 15, 1 Stat. 124.
61. 165 U.S. 275 at 281 (1897).
62. In *Mills* v. *Alabama*, 384 U.S. 214 at 219 (1966), the Court stated that "Whatever differences may exist about interpretations of the First Amendment, there is practically universal agreement that a major purpose of that Amendment was to protect the free discussion of governmental affairs."
63. *Roth* v. *United States*, 354 U.S. 476 at 484 (1957).
64. Justice Holmes dissenting opinion in *Abrams* v. *United States*, 250 U.S. 616 at 630 (1919).
65. *Terminiello* v. *Chicago*, 337 U.S. 1 at 4 (1949).
66. *Roth* at 484 (1957).
67. *Stromberg* v. *California*, 283 U.S. 359 at 369 (1931).
68. Justice Brandeis in a concurring opinion to *Whitney* v. *California*, 274 U.S. 357 at 375–376 (1927).
69. *Whitney* at 375 (1927).
70. *Whitney* at 375 (1927).
71. *Roth* at 484 (1957).
72. *Chaplinsky* v. *New Hampshire*, 315 U.S. 568 at 571–572 (1942).
73. *Cox* v. *Louisiana*, 379 U.S. 536 at 554 (1965).
74. "Subject to sections 107 through 118, the owner of copyright under this title has the exclusive rights to do and to authorize any of the following. . . . " 17 U.S.C. 106.
75. *Baker* v. *Selden*, 101 U.S. 99 (1879).
76. 345 F. Supp. 108
77. Ibid. at 115.
78. 562 F. 2d 1157.
79. Ibid. at 1171.
80. 293 F. Supp. 130.
81. Ibid. at 146.
82. 672 F.2d 1095.

Part II
Technology and Copyright
in Libraries and Classrooms

4
Fair Use: The Basics

- *What is the most significant limitation on a copyright holder's exclusive rights?*
- *What factors do the courts use to determine whether or not a use is a fair one?*
- *Does the fact that a work is unpublished in itself bar a finding of fair use?*
- *How should you handle material on the Internet that does not have a copyright notice?*

Educators, librarians, and researchers are free to use the facts and ideas in a work without permission of the copyright owner (see Chapter 3). To copy the copyright owner's expression, however, the work must be in the public domain or the use must qualify as "fair use." But what exactly is fair use?

The copyright law of the United States, in Section 106, gives a bundle of rights to the copyright holder, but the law also grants certain exemptions from liability to certain users who, without these exemptions in the law, would be committing acts of copyright infringement. The exemption that this chapter will examine is that of fair use.

Before beginning the examination of fair use as embodied in Section 107 of the copyright law, the reader might find it helpful to read Section 106, in Appendix B. Section 106 details the bundle of exclusive rights that a copyright holder obtains with a copyright. Because of the rights granted in Section 106 there are a number of circumstances under which a person needing to use another's work must seek and obtain the permission of the copyright owner (the author or the publisher, in most cases).

In situations where such permissions are needed, teachers, librarians, and researchers may find it necessary to seek these permissions themselves. At colleges and universities where the bookstore is a member of the National Association of College Stores, the Copyright Clearance Center handles permissions requests for faculty. On campuses where there is a commercial copy service affiliated with the university, that service usually seeks permissions for reproducing copyrighted materials at the request of faculty and adds any permissions fees to the cost of reproduction of the material. Permission, however obtained, must be in writing, whether the permission is free or for a fee. In those cases where the fair use exemption applies, however, it is *not* necessary for the user to obtain the copyright holder's permission to use a work.

While there is no standard definition of the term "fair use," it can be described as a limitation on the exclusive rights of a copyright holder which allows someone other than the copyright holder, without prior permission, to use portions of the copyrighted work under the conditions and for the uses defined in Section 107. A common example is that of the college student who, as part of doing research for a paper, photocopies a page from a journal article in the college library. While the definition and example given here are simple, the reader is warned that the fair use doctrine is, in fact, intricate, controversial, and subject to myriad interpretations.

Fair use is an unsettled area of copyright law. For example, the *Intellectual Property and the National Information Infrastructure* report states:

> The most significant and, perhaps, murky of the limitations on a copyright owner's exclusive rights is the doctrine of fair use. . . . It is potentially available with respect to all manners of unauthorized use of all types of works in all media. When it exists, the user is not required to seek permission from the copyright owner or to pay a license fee for the use.[1]

Early cases involving this copyright exemption simply entailed determining whether or not quoting a work or paraphrasing part of a work was fair use in a given instance. While this kind of case may still arise, the arrival of a number of new technologies has brought fair use forward as a "hot" topic because there are few court cases to use as guides and because there are no guidelines available that carry the weight of the *Agreement on Guidelines for Classroom Copying in Not-for-Profit Educational Institutions with Respect to Books and Periodicals*. The technology available to schools, universities, and libraries makes it relatively simple to copy material that exists in either print or another format into a different format. For example, it's easy to scan a printed document into a computer, to download a document onto a disk, to forward a document found on the Internet to another person, or to make a copy of a chapter in a book on a copy machine. It's easy, but is it legal? Because fair use always involves a judgment call on the part of the person choosing it, anyone who may be involved with the doctrine should be as thoroughly familiar as possible with the fair use provisions of the law and the cases that have been decided. After becoming familiar with the basics, educators and librarians should read their professional journals to keep abreast of relevant cases and ongoing developments in the law.

Section 107, *Limitations on exclusive rights: Fair use*, contains the most significant limitation on a copyright holder's exclusive rights. This doctrine of fair use is now a part of the United States copyright law, codified as Section 107 of Title 17 of the United States Code. Prior to the passage of the 1976 law which became effective on January 1, 1978, and under which this country now operates, fair use was something that the courts developed and recognized for certain special circumstances.

Under the doctrine of fair use, Section 107 of the copyright law, it is not necessary to seek the copyright holder's permission to use the author's material under certain circumstances.

Section 107 states that:

Notwithstanding the provisions of sections 106 and 106A, the fair use of a copyrighted work, including such use by reproduction in copies or phonorecords or by any other means specified by that section, for purposes such as criticism, comment, news reporting, teaching (including multiple copies for classroom use), scholarship, or research, is not an infringement of copyright.

The legislative history of the 1976 act, embodied in House Report 94–1476, notes that the reference to fair use

"by reproduction in copies or phonorecords or by any other means" is mainly intended to make clear that the doctrine has as much application to photocopying and taping as to older forms of use; it is not intended to give these kinds of reproduction any special status under the reasonable limits of fair use.

Congress clearly was aware that older forms of duplication were now superseded by the new technology of the time, and that still newer technology ("reproduction . . . by any other means . . . ") was anticipated. Consequently, it is appropriate to assume that today's technologies are not precluded from application in the fair use arena.

Note that fair use is "for purposes such as criticism, comment, news reporting, teaching . . . , scholarship, or research," which indicates that there may be other purposes for which a use could be fair. It should also be noted that it cannot be presumed that a use for one of the purposes as listed in 107 will always be found to be fair.

Fair use is an affirmative defense to an action for copyright infringement. This means that a copyright holder need not prove that a use was not fair, but that the defendant must prove it was fair. To avoid liability, a defendant bears the burden of bringing forward the evidence and of persuading the court.

Since copyright law is federal law, the reader should be aware that an infringement suit is processed through the federal court system. The initial suit would be brought at the District Court level. The side that loses at the District Court level may then appeal to the appropriate Circuit Court of Appeals. The loser of the appeal may seek relief from the United States Supreme Court, although that Court could choose not to take the case, leaving the earlier decision of a lower court intact.

In cases where an infringement suit is brought against an alleged infringer by the copyright holder, the courts look at four factors to determine whether or not the use was a fair one.

These factors are:

(1) the purpose and the character of the use, including whether such use is of a commercial nature or is for nonprofit educational purposes
(2) the nature of the copyrighted work
(3) the amount and substantiality of the portion used in relation to the copyrighted work as a whole
(4) the effect of the use on the potential market for or value of the copyrighted work

The fact that a work is unpublished shall not itself bar a finding of fair use if such finding is made upon consideration of all the above factors.

In 1975 one of the most famous library photocopying cases was decided while Congress was working on the Copyright Law of 1976. In *Williams & Wilkins Co.* v. *United States* [2] a major publisher of medical journals sued a federal medical research organization and its library for copyright infringement of four of its journals. The library photocopied articles from the medical journals at the request of researchers and medical practitioners and made interlibrary loans. The copying was massive, involving 93,000 articles in 1970 alone. The library restricted copying on individual requests to a single copy of a single article and to articles of fewer than 50 pages. Interlibrary loans were made only if an article was at least five years old or was not from one of the 100 journals considered to be widely available.[3] The Court's analysis in this case, as well as in several more recent cases to be described herein, is helpful in understanding how the four factors and other considerations are used by the courts to reach a conclusion as to whether or not a use has been a fair one. In *Williams* the Court:

1. Noted that the copying was for a noncommercial purpose and was for a limited class of requesters.
2. Noted that the copying was from two areas of research—science and education—that depended greatly on past works.
3. Noted that the requests normally were limited to single articles of 50 pages or less. Even though the copy was of an entire article, it could be considered a discreet whole, not the entire journal.
4. Found the effect on the market to be minimal. The medical publisher failed to show that it had been substantially harmed by the library's practices.

The first factor, the purpose and character of the use, continues to play an important part in the decision of whether or not a use is fair. For example, in the case of *Sony* v. *Universal City Studios, Inc.*,[4] the U.S. Supreme Court decided that taping a program in one's home, a noncommercial use, for the purpose of time shifting (to watch the program later) was fair use. In addition to that finding, the Court in *Sony* went on to declare that all commercial uses were to be presumed unfair. However, ten years later, the Court modified that ruling in allowing a commercial fair use in the case of *Campbell* v. *Acuff-Rose Music, Inc.*[5]

In *Campbell* v. *Acuff-Rose Music, Inc.*, in looking at the character and purpose of the use, the Court found the taking of the tune "Oh, Pretty Woman" by the rock group 2 Live Crew to make a parody was a fair use, even though it was a commercial use, because of the "transformative" nature of the new work. In explaining that decision, the Court looked at the landmark *Folsom* v. *Marsh* decision and specifically considered the proposition stated therein as to whether the

> object in a case like Acuff-Rose is to see whether the new work merely "supersedes the objects" of the original creation, or instead adds something new, with a further purpose or different character, altering the first with new expression, meaning, or message; it asks, in other words, whether and to what extent the new work is "transformative."[6]

In other words, it appears that to the courts the verbatim copying of a work for a commercial purpose is not generally seen as a fair use, while a work that builds on the original may be.

Even uses that can be construed to be for nonprofit educational purposes may fail this "purpose and character" test if there is simple verbatim copying involved, since the court looks for a transformative use. For example, in the case of *Marcus* v. *Rowley*,[7] the court denied fair use to a teacher who simply reproduced the copyrighted text materials of another teacher. In the case of *Encyclopedia Britannica Educ. Corp.* v. *Crooks*,[8] the court again denied fair use to a school system's practice of taping educational broadcasts for later use in classrooms.

And, of course, there is the well-known case of *Basic Books, Inc.* v. *Kinko's Graphics Corp.*,[9] in which Kinko's, a commercial copyshop operation, claimed that their copying of articles and parts of books for college students, tailored to the specifications of the professors involved, was a transformative, educational fair use. The court did not buy that argument, finding instead that Kinko's copying was a "mere repackaging" and its purpose was to supplant the "copyright holder's commercially valuable right." After that decision, Kinko Graphics Corporation ceased putting together customized anthologies for college classroom use.

In an interesting turn of events, just as the body of this work was ready to be sent to Neal-Schuman for editing, a late-breaking case with a result opposite to the *Kinko* case emerged from the courts. In the case of *Princeton University Press, Macmillan, Inc., and St. Martin's Press, Inc.* v. *Michigan Document Services, Inc., and James M. Smith*,[10] allegation was made that the Michigan Document Service (MDS) infringed copyrights held by the plaintiff publishers when MDS made multiple copies of excerpts from items provided by University of Michigan professors and put the copies together as coursepacks for sale to students. The publishers alleged that the coursepacks did not constitute fair use for a number of reasons: they had no transformative value; they were prepared for commercial purposes; the excerpts were lengthy and constituted the heart of each work; the works excerpted were valuable, original works at the core of copyright protection; and MDS's refusal to pay permissions fees affected an established derivative market in which licensed users paid to copy excerpts of copyrighted works for a variety of purposes. The lower court (District Court) found MDS's copying for coursepacks to be an infringement.

The defendants (MDS and James M. Smith) appealed the decision to the Sixth Circuit. There, by a 2–1 majority, a panel of three judges accepted the MDS argument that the purpose of the copyright clause was not to enrich authors and inventors but to encourage the progress of science and the production of creative works for the public good. MDS pointed out that the materials selected by the professors exposed their students to theories, facts, and recent developments in the field that are most relevant to classroom goals; that the professors received no commissions or other economic benefits; and that the publishers lost no sales because the copyrighted materials in their entirety would not have been assigned.

In its analysis, in terms of the character and purpose of the use, the court found that the students and professors could copy the materials themselves under fair use. The court then noted that MDS could perform the reproduction of these materials more economically than the individuals could. Since the use of the copies was for an educational purpose, there was no requirement that the use be "transformative." So saying, the court found fair use under the first factor. As to the second factor, the nature of the copyrighted work, the Sixth Circuit Court said "[it] does little more than confirm that the works at issue are protected by copyright and may only be used 'fairly,'" and went on to look at factors three and four. As to the third factor, the amount and substantiality of the portion used in relation to the copyrighted work as a whole, there were six works copied, with the percentage of a work copied varying from 5 percent to 30 percent. On this factor, the court found that the copyrighted works were not excerpted so substantially that the coursepacks superseded the original work, and, therefore, the use was a fair one. On the fourth and, generally, most important factor, the effect of the use on the potential market for or value of the copyrighted work, again the court found fair use. The reasoning of the panel of judges was that there was no evidence that the market for the original work, or any derivatives, was affected by the copied excerpts. The publishers assumed the burden of proof to demonstrate "at least a meaningful likelihood that future harm to a potential market would occur" once the determination was made that the use had been a nonprofit educational one. They failed to satisfy the court when they could only point out that what they had lost were the fees they would have imposed for permissions, had they been sought.

When the decision of the Sixth Circuit panel was rendered, the publishers were dismayed. They immediately requested a rehearing en banc (with all judges sitting). The motion for a rehearing was granted, which automatically vacated the opinion of the panel.

Whichever side loses at the rehearing is expected to appeal the decision to the United States Supreme Court. If that court accepts the case, at last educators and copyshops may have a clearer idea of the boundaries of fair use. Because the Kinko decision (like the Texaco case discussed below) was accepted by the defendants, there was no appeal in either case to the Supreme Court, and, therefore, no nationwide precedent. A decision by the United States Supreme Court in the MDS case, however, if there is one—will take time.

In another case watched closely by librarians, researchers, and faculty members, *American Geophysical Union* v. *Texaco, Inc.*[11] the U.S. District Court for the Southern District of New York found that the photocopying of eight articles from the *Journal of Catalysis* for use by one of Texaco's researchers was not fair use. In that decision, the fact that Texaco is a for-profit organization weighed against the company on this factor.

When the case went up on appeal, the Second Circuit Court looked carefully at the fact that " . . . the link between Texaco's commercial gain and its copying is somewhat attenuated . . . " and that the copying merely facilitated the scientist's research that might have led to the production of commercially valuable products. The court also noted that generally a claimed defense of fair use will not be sustained when the secondary use can fairly be characterized as a form of "commercial exploitation." Although not finding such commercial exploitation in Texaco's actions, the court, in regard to this first factor, ultimately said, " . . . it is not obvious why it is fair for Texaco to avoid having to pay at least some price to copyright holders for the right to photocopy the original articles." Yet, Texaco might still have prevailed on this factor but for the fact that the court was looking for a transformative use as well. On that issue the court did not accept Texaco's argument that its conversion of the individual *Catalysis* articles through photocopying into a form more easily used in a laboratory was a transformative use, but found instead that the predominantly archival purpose of the copying tipped the first factor against Texaco.

In regard to the nature of the copyrighted work—the second factor—the courts have generally found for the copyright owner when the work is fiction and/or is unpublished, and for the user when the work is nonfiction and/or published.

The Supreme Court dealt with the matter of unpublished material in the case of *Salinger* v. *Random House, Inc.*[12] The distinguished scholar and biographer, Ian Hamilton, decided to write an unauthorized biography of the reclusive author J. D. Salinger. Hamilton discovered a number of letters written by Salinger, donated to and residing in the collections of the libraries of some well-known universities. The biographer quoted from these letters in his manuscript. When Salinger discovered this, he objected, with the result that Hamilton then paraphrased the letters, using less material than in the first draft. Salinger still objected and took the issue to court, disputing the biographer's claim of fair use. Even though he had not necessarily followed the strictures imposed on the use of the letters by the different universities, Hamilton won at the District Court level, but the Court of Appeals reversed, holding that the use was not fair and that Salinger should have the right to be the initial publisher of his own letters. The effect of the decision was to stop the publication of the unauthorized biography, an effect which sent a jolt throughout the library and publishing worlds. To secure the rights of scholars and others to use unpublished materials, a process that seemed at risk after the court's decision in *Salinger*, concerned parties were able, after several tries, to add to Section 107, in 1992, a phrase that specifically allows fair use for unpublished works.

It is interesting to note that in the *Kinko* case, because the materials being copied were primarily factual, the courts found for the defendant Kinko on the second factor (the nature of the copyrighted materials), although Kinko lost the case.

The third factor contains some terms that, although quantitative in nature, remain undefined. There are no absolute measures of the terms "amount" and "substantiality of the portion used in relation to the copyrighted work as a whole." But the courts have provided direction in a variety of cases.

Taking only a small amount may be found to be an infringement. The 1841 case of *Folsom* v. *Marsh*, a case that has had a profound influence on copyright, stated:

> . . . it is certainly not necessary, to constitute an invasion of copyright, that the whole of a work should be copied, or even a larger portion of it, in form or in substance. If so much is taken that the value of the original is sensibly diminished, or the labors of the original author are substantially to an injurious extent appropriated by another, that is sufficient, in point of law, to constitute *a privacy pro tanto*. . . .

Nor does it necessarily depend on the quantity taken, whether it is an infringement of the copyright or not. It is often affected by other considerations, the value of the materials taken, and the importance of it to the sale of the original work.

There are times, though, when taking all or mostly all of a work is not an infringement under the fair use analysis. The *Campbell* case, mentioned above, in which 2 Live Crew took the melody, and part of the words of "Oh, Pretty Woman" is such an example. The Supreme Court looked at the amount used in relation to the purpose of the copying, and remanded to permit evaluation of the amount taken, in light of the song's parodic purpose and character, its transformative elements, and considerations of the potential for market substitution.

It is the fourth factor, the economic effect of the use, that the courts have repeatedly identified as the most significant. This factor weighs against a defendant both when there is a current market for a work and when there appears to be a potential market.

One example arose in the case of *Harper & Row, Publishers, Inc.* v. *Nation Enterprises*[13] in which *Nation* magazine printed parts of a purloined copy of an excerpt from former President Gerald Ford's book. The publisher, Harper & Row, had previously agreed to allow *Time* magazine to print the excerpt prior to the book's publication. When *Nation* scooped *Time* by printing the information on why Ford pardoned former President Nixon, *Time* declined to pay the publisher the agreed-upon fee. Harper & Row sued *Nation*. The U.S. Supreme Court denied the *Nation* claim of fair use, stating that, "a fair use doctrine that permits extensive prepublication quotations from an unreleased manuscript without the copyright owner's consent poses substantial potential for damage to the marketability of first serialization rights in general."[14]

The case of *American Geophysical Union* v. *Texaco, Inc.* is another example of the importance of the economic impact factor in determining whether or not there is fair use. In that closely watched case, the lower court concluded that the publishers "powerfully demonstrated entitlement to prevail as to the fourth factor," since they had shown "a substantial harm to the value of their copyrights" as the consequence of Texaco's copying.[15]

The Circuit Court, in considering the *Texaco* case on appeal, looked very carefully at this economic factor. It decided that while journal publishers do not provide a service whereby someone can easily purchase individual articles from a given issue, the specific journal in the case, *Catalyst,* did have a photocopying license available at the time that the Texaco researcher was making photocopies without such an agreement. The appeals court therefore decided that, "Primarily because of lost licensing revenue, and to a minor extent because of lost subscription revenue . . . ,"[16] the fourth statutory factor favored the publishers. Although this is a Circuit Court decision, and thus not "the law of the land," it is an important ruling.

Thus far, of course, the courts have dealt with printed materials. Whether or not this same pattern of decisions, in relationship to the four factors, will be found to be applicable to works in an electronic format remains to be seen. There is some reason to believe that the courts will at least try to fit the present law to the new technologies. As the *Intellectual Property and the National Information Infrastructure* report (p. 73)[17] states in regard to fair use

> ... It is potentially available with respect to all manner of unauthorized use for all types of works in all media.

Unfortunately, a decision in regard to when someone can safely rely on the fair use exemption is not necessarily a simple one. To help assure that teachers and others do not exceed the boundaries of fair use, several sets of guidelines that have the recognition of the courts have been developed. Guidelines have also been developed by the American Library Association and other concerned groups. In addition, there are a number of statements in support of fair use, generated by a variety of entities.

ELECTRONIC NETWORKS

It seems likely that for the time being the courts will approach claims of fair use in the electronic environment of the Internet just as they approach those in the more traditional print environment. Use for a commercial purpose, particularly one that is not transformative, will probably be declared to be infringing. Use for a nonprofit educational purpose that is transformative will likely be a fair use. If past experience is any indication, the cases will not be at the extremes of the paradigm, but will instead contain enough variables to require in-depth analysis on a factor-by-factor basis on the part of the court, and much anticipation on the part of both the plaintiff and the defendant.

Those who find something of interest on the Internet or other electronic services should remember that the author, in fixing his or her ideas in a medium, establishes copyright for that material. It is there whether or not the author takes the time and spends the dollars needed to register the copyright. In addition, if the author does go to the trouble of registering his or her copyright with the copyright office, there is no longer a requirement under the law to affix a copyright notice.

Before the United States joined the Berne Convention on March 1, 1989, the copyright notice was required to protect one's rights, but now that requirement is gone. Consequently, it is best to assume that material one locates on the Internet or other networks is subject to the same fair use requirements as materials that carry a copyright notice. As with other formats, asking for and receiving permission for use of material in an electronic format is the best way to approach the issue. However, time constraints and other problems may eliminate that alternative. The user must then consider the factors that make up fair use and determine whether or not to go forward. (See the Fair Use Checklist at the end of this chapter for some aid in making that decision.)

For the time being, fair use cases already decided in other contexts must serve as guides when courts are confronted with new cases that concern the use of materials from sources such as broadcast television (including retransmission by cable), local area networks, wide area networks, commercial electronic services, the Internet, the World Wide Web, or the National Information Infrastructure. Some assumptions can be made. The courts have given the go-ahead to off-air recording for home use for the purpose of time shifting. The guidelines for educational use of off-air videotapes give nonprofit educational institutions the ability to tape broadcasts for classroom use, but with stringent timelines for use and erasure. The guidelines for classroom copying of books and periodicals furnish a model for those who seek to copy electronic sources for the same purposes and manner outlined therein. The guidelines for the educational use of music have relevance to the world of electronics and automation as well.

CONFERENCE ON FAIR USE

In 1993, President Clinton formed the Information Infrastructure Task Force (IITF) to articulate and implement the administration's vision for the National Information Infrastructure (NII). Chaired by the Secretary of Commerce, the IITF consists of high-level representatives of federal agencies that play a role in advancing the development and application of information technologies. The IITF is organized into three committees: Telecommunications Policy, Applications and Technology, and Information Policy.

The Working Group on Intellectual Property Right, chaired by Assistant Secretary of Commerce and Commissioner of Patents and Trademarks Bruce A. Lehman, was established within the Information Policy committee to examine the intellectual property implications of the NII and make recommendations on any appropriate changes to U.S. intellectual property law and policy.

In September 1995, the Working Group issued its report *Intel-*

lectual Property and the National Information Infrastructure. (The report describes the NII as an infrastructure that "encompasses digital, interactive services now available, such as the Internet, as well as those contemplated for the future." The report goes on to say that

> To make the analyses more concrete, the Working Group has, in many instances, evaluated the intellectual property implications of activity on the Internet, the superstructure whose protocols and rules effectively create (or permit the creation of) a "network of networks." This reflects neither an endorsement of the Internet nor a derogation of any other existing or proposed network or service that may be available via the NII, but rather, an acknowledgment that a currently functioning structure lends itself more readily to legal analysis than a hypothetical construct based on future developments.[18]

To determine whether or not educational or library guidelines—like those developed under fair use for classroom copying, educational uses of music, and off-air taping for classroom use—could be generated for use in the NII context, the Working Group convened a conference of more than 60 interested parties, designated as the Conference on Fair Use (CONFU). This group has met more or less monthly since September 1994 and it is anticipated that the drafts developed by the group may result in formalized guidelines in the near future. The participants are examining several areas, including multimedia, library preservation, "browsing," and "distance learning." Some of the participants in CONFU are concerned that the United States could become a nation of information "haves" and "have nots," unless there are guidelines to ensure that the fair use defense is broadly interpreted in a networked environment. Until guidelines appear, teachers, faculty member, researchers, and librarians must look to existing court decisions, the various official and unofficial guidelines, and the law itself in determining for themselves what constitutes fair use in the electronic context. If the CONFU participants can't agree on a set of guidelines, it is possible the Working Group may recommend legislative action to deal with the issues under consideration.

THE FUTURE OF FAIR USE

While it is too soon to predict what the future holds for the fair use doctrine, there is reason for concern for those in the realms of education, research, and libraries. Licensing agreements, something relatively new to professionals in these fields, are attached to many electronic information resources. Written by vendors' counsel, these agreements look after the vendors' interests very well. Those in the fields of education, research, and libraries, however, often lack access to legal advice as to the viability of the licenses and contracts, in terms of their own or their users' needs. While the doctrine of fair use coexists with the licenses and contracts, the tendency among educators, researchers, and librarians is to stay safely within the terms of any agreements, some of which are quite restrictive.

The Working Group report points out that technology presents owners of copyrighted electronic works with the capability (through methods such as encryption, digital signatures, and digital watermarking or steganography) to prevent use except by paying customers—in effect, building a wall around the information. Even a cursory look at an index of librarians' professional publications can turn up a number of articles that ask the question, "Is fair use dead?"

The case of *American Geophysical Union* v. *Texaco, Inc.* illustrates that the courts—at least in the context of the for-profit sector—look at the availability of a licensing system as a rationale to reduce the application and scope of fair use. The court speculated in that case that if the copyright holder had no licensing system in place, then the balance might have shifted in favor of a finding of fair use.

Because of this concern about the possible erosion of the doctrine of fair use, library groups are finding it necessary to write position papers regarding, or including, the issue. Two examples are the statement of principles put out by the Association of Research Libraries and the statement on fair use in the electronic age, a working document developed by representatives from the American Association of Law Libraries, the American Library Association (ALA), the Association of Academic Health Sciences Library Directors, the Association of Research Libraries, the Medical Library Association (MLA), and the Special Libraries Association (SLA); endorsed by the Art Libraries Society of North America; and approved in principle by ALA.

The first document, entitled *Intellectual Property: An Association of Research Libraries Statement of Principles* (see Appendix G) contains seven principles, the first five of which are particularly relevant to the issue of fair use. Those five are

> *Principle 1*: Copyright exists for the public good. The United States copyright law is founded on a constitutional provision intended to "promote

the progress of Science and Useful Arts." The fundamental purpose of copyright is to serve the public interest by encouraging the advancement of knowledge through a system of exclusive but limited rights for authors and copyright owners. Fair use and other public rights to utilize copyrighted works, specifically and intentionally included in the 1976 revision of the law, provide the essential balance between the rights of authors, publishers, and copyright owners, and society's interest in the free exchange of ideas.[19]

Principle 2: Fair use, the library, and other relevant provisions of the Copyright Act of 1976 must be preserved in the development of the emerging information infrastructure. Fair use and other relevant provisions are the essential means by which teachers teach, students learn, and researchers advance knowledge. The Copyright Act of 1976 defines intellectual property principles in a way that is independent of the form of publication or distribution. These provisions apply to all formats and are essential to modern library and information services.

Principle 3: As trustees of the rapidly growing record of human knowledge, libraries and archives must have full use of technology in order to preserve our heritage of scholarship and research. Digital works of enduring value need to be preserved just as printed works have long been preserved by research libraries. Archival responsibilities have traditionally been undertaken by libraries because publishers and database producers have generally preserved particular knowledge only as long as it has economic value in the marketplace. As with other formats, the preservation of electronic information will be the responsibility of libraries and they will continue to perform this important societal role. The policy framework of the emerging information infrastructure must provide for the archiving of electronic materials by research libraries to maintain permanent collections and environments for public access. Accomplishing this goal will require strengthening the library provisions of the copyright law to allow preservation activities that use electronic and other appropriate technologies as they emerge.

Principle 4: Licensing agreements should not be allowed to abrogate the fair use and library provisions authorized in the copyright statute. Licenses may define the rights and privileges of the contracting parties differently from those defined by the Copyright Act of 1976. But licenses and contracts should not negate fair use and the public right to utilize copyrighted works. The research library community recognizes that there will be a variety of payment methods for the purchase of copyrighted materials in electronic formats, just as there are differing contractual agreements for acquiring printed information. The research library community is committed to working with publishers and database producers to develop model agreements that deploy licenses that do not contract around fair use and other copyright provisions.

Principle 5: Librarians and educators have an obligation to educate information users about their rights and responsibilities under intellectual property law. Institutions of learning must continue to employ policies and procedures that encourage copyright compliance. For example, the Copyright Act of 1976 required the posting of copyright notices on photocopy equipment. This practice should be updated to other technologies which permit the duplication of copyrighted works.

The second document is titled *Fair Use in the Electronic Age: Serving the Public Interest* and is labeled as a working document from the library community, dated January 18, 1995. It states:

The genius of United States copyright law is that, in conformance with its constitutional foundation, it balances the intellectual property interests of authors, publishers and copyright owners with society's need for the free exchange of ideas. Taken together, fair use and other public rights to utilize copyrighted works, as confirmed in the Copyright Act of 1976, constitute indispensable legal doctrines for promoting the dissemination of knowledge, while ensuring authors, publishers and copyright owners appropriate protection of their creative works and economic investments. The fair use provision of the Copyright Act allows reproduction and other uses of copyrighted works under certain conditions for purposes such as criticism, comment, news reporting, teaching (including multiple copies for classroom use), scholarship or research. Additional provisions of the law allow uses specifically permitted by Congress to further educational and library activities. The preservation and continuation of these balanced rights in an electronic environment as well as in traditional formats are essential to the free flow of information and to the development of an information infrastructure that serves the public interest.

It follows that the benefits of the new technologies should flow to the public as well as to copyright proprietors. As more information becomes available only in electronic formats, the public's legitimate right to use copyrighted material must be protected. In order for copyright to truly serve its purpose of "promoting progress," the public's right of fair use must continue in the electronic era, and these lawful uses of copyrighted works must be allowed without individual transaction fees. Without infringing copyright, the public has a right to expect:

- to read, listen to, or view publicly marketed copyrighted material privately, on site or remotely;
- to browse through publicly marketed copyrighted material;
- to experiment with variations of copyrighted material for fair use purposes, while preserving the integrity of the original;
- to make or have made for them a first generation copy for personal use of an article or other small part of a publicly marketed copyrighted work or a work in a library's collection for such purpose as study, scholarship, or research; and to make transitory

copies if ephemeral or incidental to a lawful use and if retained only temporarily.

Without infringing copyright, nonprofit libraries and other Section 108 libraries, on behalf of their clientele, should be able:

- to use electronic technologies to preserve copyrighted materials in their collections;
- to provide copyrighted materials as part of electronic reserve room service;
- to provide copyrighted materials as part of electronic interlibrary loan service; and
- to avoid liability, after posting appropriate copyright notices, for the unsupervised actions of their users.

Users, libraries, and educational institutions have a right to expect:

- that the terms of licenses will not restrict fair use or other lawful library or educational uses;
- that U.S. government works and other public domain materials will be readily available without restrictions and at a government price not exceeding the marginal cost of dissemination; and
- that rights of use for nonprofit education apply in face-to-face teaching and in transmittal or broadcast to remote locations where educational institutions of the future must increasingly reach their students.

Carefully constructed copyright guidelines and practices have emerged for the print environment to ensure that there is a balance between the rights of users and those of authors, publishers, and copyright owners. New understandings, developed by all stakeholders, will help to ensure that this balance is retained in a rapidly changing electronic environment. This working statement addresses lawful uses of copyrighted works in both the print and electronic environments.

FAIR USE CHECKLIST

It is important that school administrators and teachers, university administrators and faculty, researchers, and library administrators and librarians become familiar with the fair use provisions of the copyright law, relevant court decisions and those guidelines endorsed by Congress. It is also helpful to have some reminders when a decision must be made regarding a use that is intended to be covered under the fair use provisions. To that end, the authors have generated the Fair Use Checklist in Table 6. It is hoped that these questions will be helpful in arriving at a decision about whether or not a use is likely to be a fair use.

TABLE 6   Fair Use Checklist

Part A

__ Is there reason to believe the work is in the public domain?

If the answer is "yes," double check, then use freely if that is the case. Fair use is not an issue under these circumstances.

Part B

__ Does the owner of the work impose restrictions on the work that would preclude use without the copyright holder's permission?

If the answer is "yes," observe those restrictions. Usually, in such instances, there is a form that the researcher or scholar signs to indicate agreement to abide by the rules of the institution holding the material. If the copyright holder challenges the use, the courts look unfavorably upon the scholar who signs such an agreement but then fails to uphold it.

Part C

Below is a list of questions that should be considered by any individual who plans to invoke the fair use doctrine in regard to the use of a copyrighted resource. As indicated by the court cases, a use that is of a nonprofit, educational nature is more likely to be considered noninfringing than one that is of a commercial nature. A use that is for criticism, comment, news reporting, teaching, scholarship, or research is more likely than not to be considered a fair use. A transformative use is favored over mere copying. While taking the whole work is seldom safe, taking only a small portion that constitutes the "heart of the work" can be just as dangerous. Workbooks and other consumables *cannot* be copied under the fair use doctrine. Copying may not be done to develop anthologies or collective works. The following checklist is meant to be used as a guide and reminder of the factors that the courts have noted in the past. There may be other factors at play in a specific situation that are not covered by these questions. It is well to remember that fair use challenges are always judged on a case-by-case basis, with the specific facts in a particular case being of utmost importance.

__ Is there reason to believe that the work is under copyright?

__ Is the use for the purpose of criticism, comment, news reporting, teaching (including multiple copies for classroom use), scholarship, or research (after the *Acuff-Rose* decision, perhaps parody should be added to this list)?

__ Is there an immediate need for the use, leaving not enough time to seek permission?

__ Does the format allow copying part of the work?

__ How much of the work is to be used? What proportion?

__ Is the part to be used "the heart" of the work?

__ Is the use of a nonprofit educational nature?

__ Is the use transformative?

__ Is the work published?

__ Is the work unpublished?

__ Is the work fiction?

__ Is the work nonfiction?

__ Is the work to be quoted?

__ Is the work to be paraphrased?

__ Is there a current market for the work?

__ Is there a potential market for the work?

__ Will the use enhance the economic interests of the copyright owner?

__ Will the use harm the economic interests of the copyright holder?

__ Is the use of a commercial nature?

__ Is the use "mere reproduction"?

__ Is the use for the creation of an anthology or collective work?

__ Is the material to be used a consumable, such as a workbook?

ENDNOTES

1. P. 73.
2. 487 F. 2d 1345, aff'd, 420 U.S. 376 (1975).
3. *Encyclopedia Britannica, Inc. et al.* v. *Crooks*, 447 F. Supp. 243, 250–251(1978).
4. 464 U.S. 417 (1984).
5. 114 S. Ct. 1164 (1994).
6. *Folsom*, 348)
7. 695 F. 2d 1171 (9th Cir. 1983)
8. 558 F. Supp. 1247 (W.D.N.Y. 1983).
9. 758 F. Supp. 1522 (S.D.N.Y. 1991).
10. Electronic citation: 1996 Fed App. 0046P (6th Cir.).
11. 802 F. Supp. 1 (S.D.N.Y. 1992).
12. 811 F.2d 90 (2d Cir. 1987).
13. 471 U.S. 539 (1985).
14. *Harper & Row Publishers, Inc.* v. *National Enterprises*, 371 U.S. 539 at 557 (1985), p. 111.
15. 37F 3d 881 at 886 (2d Circuit 1994).
16. Ibid.
17. *Intellectual Property and the National Information Infrastructure.* The Report of the Working Group on Intellectual Property Rights, Bruce A. Lehman, Chair 1995, p. 73.
18. Ibid, p. 2.
19. *Intellectual Property: An Association of Research Libraries Statement of Principles,* http://avl.cn1.org/scom/copyright/principles/html/

5

Fair Use: Technology in and for the Classroom

- *Do the* Guidelines for Educational Fair Use *carry any weight with the courts?*
- *Why does the ALA* Model Policy *differ from the guidelines?*
- *When is it* not *necessary to get a copyright owner's permission to copy for classroom use?*

Section 107 of the copyright law has a number of provisions that are important for teachers, including college and university faculty, and for librarians as well. School library media specialists and academic librarians should become familiar with the rules governing copying by and for teachers and faculty members. Often, library staff members actually do the copying that a teacher or faculty member requires.

Because fair use is a somewhat vague concept, concerned groups were eager to have guidelines that were more clearly defined than the law itself. Representatives from the Ad Hoc Committee of Educational Institutions and Organizations on Copyright Revision; the Authors League of America; and the Association of American Publishers came together and agreed upon guidelines that have been given heavy weight in the courts. The *Guidelines for Educational Fair Use*, part of a House Report,[1] are for classroom copying in nonprofit educational institutions and apply to the copying of both books and periodicals. It is important to note that the guidelines state the minimum and not the maximum standards of educational fair use. It is also important to note that the conditions determining the extent of permissible copying for educational purposes may change in the future. Uses that are permissible now may not be permissible in the future and vice versa.

GUIDELINES FOR EDUCATIONAL FAIR USE

The *Guidelines for Educational Fair Use* include the following provisions:

Teachers may make a single copy for themselves, for research or teaching purposes, including preparation for teaching, of

- a chapter in a book
- an article from a periodical or newspaper
- a short story, short essay, or short poem, whether or not it is from a collective work
- a chart, graph, diagram, drawing, cartoon, or picture from a book, periodical, or newspaper.

Teachers and faculty members have certain privileges in regard to making copies for their students. Teachers and faculty can make multiple copies (one copy for each pupil, that is) for classroom use if the copying meets three tests, and if the copies carry a notice of copyright. The three tests are for brevity, spontaneity, and cumulative effect.

Brevity is defined as

- a complete poem if less than 250 words and if printed on not more than two pages, or an excerpt from a poem of not more than 250 words
- a complete article, story, or essay of less than 2,500 words or an excerpt of not more than 1,000 words or 10 percent of a work, whichever is less, but in any event a *minimum* of 500 words
- one chart, graph, diagram, drawing, cartoon, or picture per book or per periodical issue.
- not more than two published pages containing less than 10 percent of the words found in the text of "special works" (special works are those that combine language—such as poetry, prose, or poetic prose— and illustrations and which have fewer than a total of 2,500 words; they may or may not be children's materials)

The spontaneity test demands that

- the copying be by or at the direction of the individual teacher
- there be too short a time between discovery of material and the day that it must be used in the classroom to ask for and receive permission

Cumulative effect requires that

- the copying be for only one course in the school where the copies are made
- only one short poem, article, story, essay, or two excerpts may be copied from the same author, and not more than three from the same collective work or periodical volume during one class term
- there shall be no more than nine instances of multiple copying for one course during one class term

The strictures on what may be copied and the limit of nine instances do not apply to current news periodicals, newspapers and current news sections of other periodicals.

In regard to single copying for teachers and multiple copies for classroom use, there are further prohibitions which include:

- Copies may not be used to create, replace, or substitute for anthologies, compilations, or collective works.
- Consumable materials, including workbooks, exercises, standardized tests, and answer sheets are prohibited from being copied.
- Copying must be requested by the classroom teacher and cannot be directed by higher authority.
- Copying cannot be repeated "with respect to the same item by the same teacher from term to term."
- The student may not be charged, if there is a charge, more than the actual costs of photocopying.

In general, these guidelines are in effect in the school systems across America and in many colleges and universities. While the preamble to the guidelines states that, "There may be instances in which copying which does not fall within the guidelines ... may nonetheless be permitted under the criteria of fair use,"[2] most teachers or faculty members are unwilling to risk being a test case.

Of course, a school system, college, or university should have a copyright policy in place, with the adoption of these guidelines, or something similar, as part of that policy. While these guidelines do have wide acceptance, it should be remembered that the American Association of University Professors and the Association of American Law Schools declined to endorse them, finding them too restrictive for higher education.

To address the fact that there was no university faculty representation in the development of the guidelines for educational fair use, in 1982 the American Library Association (ALA) issued a *Model Policy Concerning College and University Photocopying for Classroom Research and Library Reserve Use*. In regard to classroom copying, this model policy recommends that "the standard guidelines should be followed." However, the policy goes on to say that the standard guidelines set minimum standards for photocopying that "normally would not be realistic in the University setting . . . " and that "faculty members needing to exceed these limits for college education should not feel hampered by these guidelines, although they should attempt a 'selective and sparing' use of photocopied, copyrighted material."[3]

The policy points out that:

> Too often, members of the academic community have been reluctant or hesitant to exercise their rights of fair use under the law for fear of courting an infringement suit. It is important to understand that in U.S. law, copyright is a limited statutory monopoly and the public's right to use materials must be protected. Safeguards have been written into the legislative history accompanying the new copyright law protecting librarians, teachers, researchers and scholars and guaranteeing their rights of access to information as they carry out their responsibilities for educating or conducting research. It is, therefore, important to heed the advise of a former U.S. Register of Copyrights: "If you don't use fair use, you will lose it!"

The ALA policy includes examples of situations where increased levels of photocopying would remain within the ambit of fair use. These situations include:

- the inability to obtain another copy of the work because it is not available from another library or because the source cannot be obtained within the user's time constraints
- the intention to photocopy the material only once and not to distribute the material to others
- the ability to keep the amount of material photocopied within a reasonable proportion to the entire work (the larger the work, the greater amount of material that may be photocopied). Most single-copy photocopying for a faculty member's personal use in research—even when it involves a substantial portion of a work—may well constitute fair use.

While it is important to know that the standard guidelines indicate the minimum rather than the maximum copying that can be considered fair use, appropriate restraint is advised. In a 1983 incident that created great interest in the academic community, New York University agreed to adopt the standard guidelines as part of its copyright policy when challenged by the Association of American Publishers about exceeding them. Widely publicized, this incident undoubtedly had an effect on the copying activities and policies of other colleges and universities.

GUIDELINES FOR THE EDUCATIONAL USE OF MUSIC

While a group of interested parties was developing guidelines for classroom copying in a nonprofit educational institution, another group was working on guidelines for the educational use of music.

As with any copyrighted material, when one wishes to copy, modify, or otherwise embellish printed music, the first course of action is to seek permission from the copyright holder. Permissions should always be in writing. The world of music functions somewhat differently from the world of publishing. ASCAP (the American Society of Composers, Artists and Publishers) and BMI (Broadcast Music, Incorporated) have licensed music and collected royalty for years.

When there are time constraints or other good reasons for not getting permission, educators have certain privileges under the guidelines established for the educational uses of printed music. These guidelines were developed through a cooperative effort of the Music Publishers' Association of the United States, the Music Teachers National Association, the Music Education National Conference, the National Association of Schools of Music, and the Ad Hoc Committee on Copyright Law Revision. Representatives from these groups met and developed permissible uses regarding printed music. These guidelines state the minimum, not the maximum, standards of educational fair use (Section 107 of the U.S. Copyright Act) in effect at the present time. Over time, the conditions that determine the extent of permissible copying of music for educational purposes may change, making certain types of copying now permitted impermissible in the future and, conversely, making presently impermissible copying possible. It is, therefore, important for concerned parties to keep current on developments in this area of the law. Generally, the commonly read professional journals carry news of pertinent changes in the copyright law.

There may also be instances when copying that doesn't fall within the guidelines for the educational use of music may be permitted under the criteria of fair use under judicial decision; so it is essential to know the criteria and to check with legal counsel if there is doubt as to the advisability of a particular course of action.

The guidelines for the educational uses of music allow for the following:[4]

1. Emergency copying to replace purchased copies that for any reason are not available for *an imminent performance, provided that purchased replacement copies shall be substituted in due course.*
2. For academic purposes other than performance, single or multiple

copies of excerpts of works may be made, provided that the excerpts do not comprise a part of the whole that would constitute a performable unit such as a section, movement, or aria, *but* in no case more than 10 percent of the whole work (the number of copies shall not exceed one copy per pupil).

3. Printed copies that have been purchased may be edited or simplified provided that the fundamental character of the work is not distorted, or the lyrics, if any, are not altered, or lyrics are not added if none exist.

4. A single copy of recordings of performances by students may be made for evaluation or rehearsal purposes and may be retained by the educational institution or individual teacher.

5. A single copy of a sound recording (such as a tape, disk, or cassette) of copyrighted music may be made from sound recordings owned by an educational institution or an individual teacher for the purpose of constructing aural exercises or examinations and may be retained by the educational institution or individual teacher. This proviso pertains only to the copyright of the music itself and not to any copyright that may exist in the sound recording.

While these permissible uses seem to be expressed in a straightforward way, note that in the first item the key phrase "in due course" is an undefined time period in which "purchased replacement copies shall be substituted" for the emergency copies made for an imminent performance. Because of this lack of definition, the best advice that can be given is that the phrase "in due course" should be interpreted as meaning "as quickly as possible."

Another important but undefined term appears in the third item. The editing allowed in that permissible use is only that which does not distort the "fundamental character." Since there is no definition of "fundamental character," the safest course is to edit minimally, if at all.

General prohibitions exist in regard to these guidelines, including:[5]

1. The copying may *not* be used to create, replace, or substitute for anthologies, compilations, or collective works.

2. The copying may not be of or from works intended to be "consumable" in the course of study or of teaching, such as workbooks, exercises, standardized tests and answer sheets, and like material.

3. Copying for the purpose of performance is prohibited, except in the emergency situation described above.

4. Copying as a way of avoiding purchase is forbidden, given the reasonable availability of the material.

5. No copying is permitted unless the copyright notice that appears on the printed music is included.

CLASSROOM USE OF OFF-AIR VIDEOTAPES

Another set of guidelines that was developed under the fair use doctrine is that for classroom use of off-air videotapes. In the spring of 1979, Democratic Representative Robert Kastenmeier of Wisconsin brought together 19 educational users and copyright proprietors as a committee for the purpose of writing off-air recording guidelines, which were then published in the *Congressional Record.*

These guidelines, developed under the fair use doctrine, make it possible for a teacher or faculty member to record a program or to request that someone else do it, for use in the classroom. There are some restrictions:

1. The educational institution for which the recording is made must be nonprofit.
2. The educational institution is expected to establish procedures intended to maintain the integrity of the guidelines.
3. Off-air recordings cannot be regularly made in anticipation of possible requests.
4. The recording must include the copyright notice as broadcast.
5. Recording of a program off-air can be done or requested only once by the same teacher no matter how many times the program is actually broadcast.
6. The use must take place in a classroom or similar place devoted to instruction.
7. The classroom or similar place of instruction must be within a single building, cluster, or campus, or in the home of a student receiving formalized home instruction.
8. The videotape may be viewed, in whole or in part, once by each class in the course of relevant teaching activities, and one more time for instructional reinforcement, if needed.
9. Both the original and repeat performances must take place within ten consecutive school-session days from the day of the recording. Vacations, weekends, holidays, exam periods, and the like do not count in calculating the ten-day period.
10. The videotape must be erased or destroyed within 45 consecutive calendar days after the recording.
11. After the classroom use period of ten consecutive school days passes, the off-air videotape may be used during the remainder of the 45-consecutive-days retention period only for teacher evaluation as to its value to the curriculum and whether or not it should be purchased, if available.
12. The original contents of the off-air program cannot be altered, or combined, or merged with other recordings.
13. Subject to all of the above guidelines, a limited number of copies of an off-air videotape may be made to meet the legitimate needs of individual teachers.[6]

These guidelines speak clearly to a question that often comes up in copyright workshops—can the school or college library become the depository for teachers' off-air videotapes, so that they can be shared by the faculty in the particular school or college? The answer is clearly "no."

Obviously, it is important that all concerned in the nonprofit educational sector—educators, media specialists, librarians, administrators—know what the law and the guidelines permit. Also, there must be appropriate control procedures to maintain the integrity of both the law and the guidelines.

MULTIMEDIA

With today's technology, it is relatively easy to digitally combine pieces of videos, audiotapes, photographs, and printed material to generate a new work. It is safest, as in any situation where copying of copyrighted materials is planned, to obtain permissions for such use. However, under the right circumstances, the fair use umbrella can serve as a protection for the generation of such a combination.

On July 17, 1996, the Consortium of College and University Media Centers issued guidelines, which had been distributed in several draft forms for comment, on fair use of copyrighted materials by educators. These guidelines, printed in Table 7, allow students to use, under the fair use doctrine, lawfully acquired copyrighted materials in multimedia programs for educational purposes and allow the students to retain the material for such uses as seeking employment or applying to graduate school. In face-to-face teaching situations, educators may show students how to produce multimedia programs and may produce multimedia programs themselves as teaching tools. In addition, educators may exchange displays with colleagues of the multimedia programs they have created. They may use their own programs, with some restrictions, over their own institution's electronic network for remote instruction. Specific limitations are included in the guidelines on the amount of material that may be used from motion media, text, music, lyrics, music video, illustrations, photographs, and numerical data-set formats. Use under the fair use doctrine is limited to a two-year period, after which permissions must be sought. The guidelines give examples for situations in which permissions must be secured:

1. For commercial reproduction and distribution;
2. For replication or distribution beyond the limitations spelled out;
3. For use over electronic networks where access is uncontrolled.

A section on "Important Reminders" includes the caveats that:

1. Materials found on the Internet must be used with caution since they may be copyrighted;
2. Proper attribution must always be given;
3. Notice of a program's adherence to the multimedia guidelines should appear on the first screen;
4. Those creating multimedia programs which have a potential to be either broadly and/or commercially disseminated should seek permissions while the program is under development; and
5. The integrity of the original work should be maintained, with alterations being made only in support of specific instructional objectives;
6. Reproduction or decompilation of copyrighted computer programs is not permitted; and
7. License or contract terms should be respected.

The guidelines, printed in their entirety in Table 7, should be carefully read by all educators, library media specialists, and educational administrators.

It is important to realize that draft guidelines do not carry the weight of law. Indeed, many such guidelines currently being distributed in the library and educational communities are the subject of much disagreement. For example, the American Library Association's Executive Board voted on November 4, 1996, not to endorse copyright guidelines which do not fully protect the public's fair use rights. We encourage you to follow the development of these and similar guidelines closely.

TABLE 7   Fair Use Guidelines for Educational Multimedia*

July 17, 1996
Table of Contents

1. Introduction
2. Preparation of Educational Multimedia Projects Under These Guidelines
3. Permitted Educational Uses for Multimedia Projects Under These Guidelines
4. Limitations
5. Examples of When Permission Is Required
6. Important Reminders

1. Introduction

1.1 Preamble

Fair use is a legal principle that provides certain limitations on the exclusive rights** of copyright holders. The purpose of these guidelines is to provide guidance on the application of fair use principles by educators, scholars and students who develop multimedia projects using portions of copyrighted works under fair use rather than by seeking authorization for non-commercial educational uses. These guidelines apply only to fair use in the context of copyright and to no other rights.

There is no simple test to determine what is fair use. Section 107 of the Copyright Act*** sets forth the four fair use factors which should be considered in each instance, based on particular facts of a given case, to determine whether a use is a "fair use": (1) the purpose and character of use, including whether such use is of a commercial nature or is for nonprofit educational purposes, (2) the nature of the copyrighted work, (3) the amount and substantiality of the portion used in relation to the copyrighted work as a whole, and (4) the effect of the use upon the potential market for or value of the copyrighted work.

---

*These guidelines shall not be read to supersede other preexisting Education Fair Use Guidelines that deal with Section 107 of the Copyright Act.
**See Section 106 of the Copyright Act.
***The Copyright Act of 1976, as amended, is codified at 17 U.S.C. Sec. 101 et seq.

While only the courts can authoritatively determine whether a particular use is fair use, these guidelines represent the participants'**** consensus of conditions under which fair use should generally apply and examples of when permission is required. Uses that exceed these guidelines may or may not be fair use. The participants also agree that the more one exceeds these guidelines, the greater the risk that fair use does not apply.

The limitations and conditions set forth in these guidelines do not apply to works in the public domain—such as U.S. Government works or works on which copyright has expired for which there are no copyright restrictions—or to works for which the individual or institution has obtained permission for the particular use. Also, license agreements may govern the uses of some works and users should refer to the applicable license terms for guidance.

The participants who developed these guidelines met for an extended period of time and the result represents their collective understanding in this complex area. Because digital technology is in a dynamic phase, there may come a time when it is necessary to review the guidelines. Nothing in these guidelines shall be construed to apply to the fair use privilege in any context outside of educational and scholarly uses of educational multimedia projects.

This Preamble is an integral part of these guidelines and should be included whenever the guidelines are reprinted or adopted by organizations and educational institutions. Users are encouraged to reproduce and distribute these guidelines freely without permission; no copyright protection of these guidelines is claimed by any person or entity.

1.2 Background

These guidelines clarify the application of fair use of copyrighted works as teaching methods are adapted to new learning environments. Educators have traditionally brought copyrighted books, videos, slides, sound recordings and other media into the classroom, along with accompanying projection and playback equipment. Multimedia creators integrated these individual instructional resources with their own original works in a meaningful way, providing compact educational tools that allow great flexibility in teaching and learning. Material is stored so that it may be retrieved in a nonlinear fashion, depending on the needs or interests of

---

****The names of the various organizations participating in this dialog appear at the end of these guidelines and clearly indicate the variety of interest groups involved, both from the standpoint of the users of copyrighted material and also from the standpoint of copyright owners.

learners. Educators can use multimedia projects to respond spontaneously to students' questions by referring quickly to relevant portions. In addition, students can use multimedia projects to pursue independent study according to their needs or at a pace appropriate to their capabilities. Educators and students want guidance about the application of fair use principles when creating their own multimedia projects to meet specific instructional objectives.

1.3 Applicability of These Guidelines

(Certain basic terms used throughout these guidelines are identified in bold and defined in this section.)

These guidelines apply to the use, without permission, of portions of lawfully acquired copyrighted works in educational multimedia projects which are created by educators or students as part of a systematic learning activity by nonprofit educational institutions. Educational multimedia projects created under these guidelines incorporate students' or educators' original material, such as course notes or commentary, together with various copyrighted media formats including but not limited to, motion media, music, text material, graphics, illustrations, photographs and digital software which are combined into an integrated presentation. Educational institutions are defined as nonprofit organizations whose primary focus is supporting research and instructional activities of educators and students for noncommercial purposes.

For the purposes of these guidelines, educators include faculty, teachers, instructors and others who engage in scholarly, research and instructional activities for educational institutions. The copyrighted works used under these guidelines are lawfully acquired if obtained by the institution or individual through lawful means such as purchase, gift or license agreement but not pirated copies. Educational multimedia projects which incorporate portions of copyrighted works under these guidelines may be used only for educational purposes in systematic learning activities including use in connection with non-commercial curriculum-based learning and teaching activities by educators to students enrolled in courses at nonprofit educational institutions or otherwise permitted under Section 3. While these guidelines refer to the creation and use of educational multimedia projects, readers are advised that in some instances other fair use guidelines such as those for off-air taping may be relevant.

2.   Preparation of Educational Multimedia Projects Using Portions of Copyrighted Works

These uses are subject to the Portion Limitations listed in Section 4. They should include proper attribution and citation as defined in Section 6.2.

2.1 By Students:

Students may incorporate portions of lawfully acquired copyrighted works when producing their own educational multimedia projects for a specific course.

2.2 By Educators for Curriculum-Based Instruction:

Educators may incorporate portions of lawfully acquired copyrighted works when producing their own educational multimedia projects for their own teaching tools in support of curriculum-based instructional activities at educational institutions.

3.   Permitted Uses of Educational Multimedia Projects Created Under These Guidelines

Uses of educational multimedia projects created under these guidelines are subject to the Time, Portion, Copying and Distribution Limitations listed in Section 4.

3.1 Student Use:

Students may perform and display their own educational multimedia projects created under Section 2 of these guidelines for educational uses in the course for which they were created and may use them in their own portfolios as examples of their academic work for later personal uses such as job and graduate school interviews.

3.2 Educator Use for Curriculum-Based Instruction:

Educators may perform and display their own educational multimedia projects created under Section 2 for curriculum-based instruction to students in the following situations:

3.2.1 for face-to-face instruction,

3.2.2 assigned to students for directed self-study,

3.2.3 for remote instruction to students enrolled in curriculum-based courses and located at remote sites,

provided over the educational institution's secure electronic network in real-time, or for after class review or directed self-study, provided there are technological limitations on access to the network and program (such as a password or PIN) and provided further that the technology prevents the making of copies of copyrighted material.

If the educational institution's network or technology used to access the program cannot prevent duplication of copyrighted material, students or educators may use the multimedia educational projects created under Section 2 of these guidelines over an otherwise secure network for a period of only 15 days after its initial real-time remote use in the course of instruction or 15 days after its assignment for directed self-study. After that period, one of the two use copies of the educational multimedia project may be placed on reserve in a learning resource center, library or similar facility for on-site use by students enrolled in the course. Students shall be advised that they are not permitted to make their own copies of the educational multimedia project.

3.3 Educator Use for Peer Conferences:

Educators may perform or display their own educational multimedia projects created under Section 2 of these guidelines in presentations to their peers, for example, at workshops and conferences.

3.4 Educator Use for Professional Portfolio

Educators may retain educational multimedia projects created under Section 2 of these guidelines in their personal portfolios for later personal uses such as tenure review or job interviews.

4. Limitations—Time, Portion, Copying and Distribution

The preparation of educational multimedia projects incorporating copyrighted works under Section 2, and the use of such projects under Section 3, are subject to the limitations noted below.

4.1 Time Limitations

Educators may use their educational multimedia projects created for educational purposes under Section 2 of these guidelines for teaching courses, for a period of up to two years after the first instructional use with a class. Use beyond that time period, even for educational purposes, requires permission for each copyrighted portion incorporated in the production. Students may use their educational multimedia projects as noted in Section 3.1.

4.2 Portion Limitations

Portion limitations mean the amount of a copyrighted work that can reasonably be used in educational multimedia projects under these guidelines regardless of the original medium from which the copyrighted works are taken. In the aggregate means the total amount of copyrighted material from a single copyrighted work that is permitted to be used in an educational multimedia project without permission under these guidelines. These limitations apply cumulatively to each educator's or student's multimedia project(s) for the same academic semester, cycle or term. All students should be instructed about the reasons for copyright protection and the need to follow these guidelines. It is understood, however, that students in kindergarten through grade six may not be able to adhere rigidly to the portion limitations in this section in their independent development of educational multimedia projects. In any event, each such project retained under Sections 3.1 and 4.3 should comply with the portion limitations in this section.

4.2.1 Motion Media

Up to 10% or 3 minutes, whichever is less, in the aggregate of a copyrighted motion media work may be reproduced or otherwise incorporated as part of an educational multimedia project created under Section 2 of these guidelines.

4.2.2 Text Material

Up to 10% or 1000 words, whichever is less, in the aggregate of a copyrighted work consisting of text material may be reproduced or otherwise incorporated as part of an educational multimedia project created under Section 2 of these guidelines. An entire poem of less than 250 words may be used, but no more than three poems by one poet, or five poems by different poets from any anthology may be used. For poems of greater length, 250 words may be used but no more than three excerpts by a poet, or five excerpts by different poets from a single anthology may be used.

4.2.3 Music, Lyrics, and Music Video

Up to 10%, but in no event more than 30 seconds, of the music and lyrics from an individual musical work (or in the aggregate of extracts from an individual work), whether the musical work is embodied in copies, or audio or audiovisual works, may be reproduced or otherwise incorporated as a part of a multimedia project created under Section 2. Any alterations to a musical work shall not change the basic melody or the fundamental character of the work.

4.2.4 Illustrations and Photographs

The reproduction or incorporation of photographs and illustrations is more difficult to define with regard to fair use because fair use usually precludes the use of an entire work. Under these guidelines a photograph or illustration may be used in its entirety but no more than 5 images by an artist or photographer may be reproduced or otherwise incorporated as part of an educational multimedia project created under Section 2. When using photographs and illustrations from a published collective work, not more than 10% or 15 images, whichever is less, may be reproduced or otherwise incorporated as part of an educational multimedia project created under Section 2.

4.2.5 Numerical Data Sets

Up to 10% or 2500 fields or cell entries, whichever is less, from a copyrighted database or data table may be reproduced or otherwise incorporated as part of an educational multimedia project created under Section 2 of these guidelines. A field entry is defined as a specific item of information, such as a name or Social Security number, in a record of a database file. A cell entry is defined as the intersection where a row and a column meet on a spreadsheet.

4.3 Copying and Distribution Limitations

Only a limited number of copies, including the original, may be made of an educator's educational multimedia project. For all of the uses permitted by Section 3, there may be no more than two use copies only one of which may be placed on reserve as described in Section 3.2.3.

An additional copy may be made for preservation purposes but may only be used or copied to replace a use copy that has been lost, stolen, or damaged. In the case of a jointly created educational multimedia project, each principal creator may retain one copy but only for the purposes described in Sections 3.3 and 3.4 for educators and in Section 3.1 for students.

5.   Examples of When Permission Is Required

5.1 Using Multimedia Projects for Non-Educational or Commercial Purposes

Educators and students must seek individual permissions (licenses) before using copyrighted works in educational multimedia projects for commercial reproduction and distribution.

5.2 Duplication of Multimedia Projects Beyond Limitations Listed in These Guidelines

Even for educational uses, educators and students must seek individual permissions for all copyrighted works incorporated in their personally created educational multimedia projects before replicating or distributing beyond the limitations listed in Section 4.3.

5.3 Distribution of Multimedia Projects Beyond Limitations Listed in These Guidelines

Educators and students may not use their personally created educational multimedia projects over electronic networks, except for uses as described in Section 3.2.3, without obtaining permissions for all copyrighted works incorporated in the program.

6.   Important Reminders

6.1 Caution in Downloading Material from the Internet

Educators and students are advised to exercise caution in using digital material downloaded from the Internet in producing their own educational multimedia projects, because there is a mix of works protected by copyright and works in the public domain on the network. Access to works on the Internet does not automatically mean that these can be reproduced and reused without permission or royalty payment and, furthermore, some copyrighted works may have been posted to the Internet without authorization of the copyright holder.

6.2 Attribution and Acknowledgement

Educators and students are reminded to credit the sources and display the copyright notice C and copyright ownership information if this is shown in the original source, for all works incorporated as part of educational multimedia projects prepared by educators and students, including those prepared under fair use. Crediting the source must adequately identify the source of the work, giving a full bibliographic description where available (including author, title, publisher, and place and date of publication). The copyright ownership information includes the copyright notice (C, year of first publication and name of the copyright holder).

The credit and copyright notice information may be combined and shown in a separate section of the educational multimedia project (e.g. credit section) except for images incorporated into the project for the uses described in Section 3.2.3. In such cases, the copyright notice and the name of the creator of the image must be incorporated into the image when, and to the extent, such information is reasonably available; credit and copyright notice information is considered "incorporated" if it is attached to the image file and appears on the screen when the image is viewed. In those cases when displaying source credits and copyright ownership information on the screen with the image would be mutually exclusive with an instructional objective (e.g. during examinations in which the source credits and/or copyright information would be relevant to the examination questions), those images may be displayed without such information being simultaneously displayed on the screen. In such cases, this information should be linked to the image in a manner compatible with such instructional objectives.

6.3 Notice of Use Restrictions

Educators and students are advised that they must include on the opening screen of their multimedia project and any accompanying print material a notice that certain materials are included under the fair use exemption of the U.S. Copyright Law and have been prepared according to the educational multimedia fair use guidelines and are restricted from further use.

6.4 Future Uses Beyond Fair Use

Educators and students are advised to note that if there is a possibility that their own educational multimedia project incorporating copyrighted works under fair use could later result in broader dissemination, whether or not as commercial product, it is strongly recommended that they take steps to obtain permissions during the development process for all copyrighted portions rather than waiting until after completion of the project.

6.5 Integrity of Copyrighted Works: Alterations

Educators and students may make alterations in the portions of the copyrighted works they incorporate as part of an educational multimedia project only if the alterations support specific instructional objectives. Educators and students are advised to note that alterations have been made.

6.6 Reproduction or Decompilation of Copyrighted Computer Programs

Educators and students should be aware that reproduction or decompilation of copyrighted computer programs and portions thereof, for example the transfer of underlying code or control mechanisms, even for educational uses, are outside the scope of these guidelines.

6.7 Licenses and Contracts

Educators and students should determine whether specific copyrighted works, or other data or information are subject to a license or contract. Fair use and these guidelines shall not preempt or supersede licenses and contractual obligations

Prepared by the Educational Multimedia Fair Use Guidelines Development Committee, July 17, 1996

ENDNOTES

1. House Report No. 94–1476 (1976).
2. *Agreement on Guidelines for Classroom Copying in Not-for-Profit Educational Institutions* House Report No. 94–1476, preamble.
3. http://www.ala.org.
4. House Judiciary Committee Report No. 94–1476.
5. Ibid.
6. *Congressional Record* (14 October 1979): E4750–E4752.

APPENDIX A: ENDORSEMENTS AND LETTERS OF SUPPORT RECEIVED AS OF SEPTEMBER 23, 1996

1. ORGANIZATIONS ENDORSING THESE GUIDELINES:
Agency for Instructional Technology (AIT)
American Association of Community Colleges (AACC)
American Society of Journalists and Authors (ASJA)
American Society of Media Photographers, Inc. (ASMP)
American Society of Composers, Authors and Publishers (ASCAP)
Association for Educational Communications and Technology (AECT)
Association for Information Media and Equipment (AIME)
Association of American Publishers (AAP)
Association of American Colleges and Universities (AAC&U)
Association of American University Presses, Inc. (AAUP)
Broadcast Music, Inc. (BMI)
Consortium of College and University Media Centers (CCUMC)
Creative Incentive Coalition (CIC)
Instructional Telecommunications Council (ITC)
Maricopa Community Colleges/Phoenix
Motion Picture Association of America (MPAA)
Music Publishers' Association of the United States (MPA)
Recording Industry Association of America (RIAA)
Software Publishers Association (SPA)

2. INDIVIDUAL COMPANIES AND INSTITUTIONS ENDORSING THESE GUIDELINES:
Houghton Mifflin
McGraw-Hill

John Wiley & Sons, Inc.
Time Warner, Inc.

3. U.S. GOVERNMENTAL AGENCIES SUPPORTING THESE GUIDELINES:

U.S. National Endowment for the Arts (NEA)

U.S. Copyright Office

ORGANIZATIONS PARTICIPATING IN GUIDELINE DEVELOPMENT:

Being a participant does not necessarily mean the organization has or will endorse these guidelines.

Agency for Instructional Technology (AIT)

American Association of Community Colleges (AACC)

American Association for Higher Education (AAHE)

American Library Association (ALA)

American Society of Journalists and Authors (ASJA)

American Society of Media Photographers (ASMP)

Artists Rights Foundation

Association of American Colleges and Universities (AAC&U)

Association of American Publishers (AAP)

     -Harvard University Press

     -Houghton Mifflin

     -McGraw-Hill

     -Simon and Schuster

     -Worth Publishers

Association of College and Research Libraries (ACRL)

Association for Educational Communications and Technology (AECT)

Association for Information Media and Equipment (AIME)

Association of Research Libraries (ARL)

Authors Guild, Inc.

Broadcast Music, Inc. (BMI)

Consortium of College and University Media Centers (CCUMC)

Copyright Clearance Center (CCC)

Creative Incentive Coalition (CIC)

Directors Guild of America (DGA)

European American Music Distributors Corp.

Educational institutions participating in guideline discussion

     -American University

     -Carnegie Mellon University

     -City College/City University of New York

     -Kent State University

     -Maricopa Community Colleges/Phoenix

     -The Pennsylvania State University

     -University of Delaware

Information Industry Association (IIA)

Instructional Telecommunications Council (ITC)

International Association of Scientific, Technical and Medical Publishers

Motion Picture Association of America (MPAA)

Music Publishers Association (MPA)

National Association of State Universities and Land-Grant Colleges(NASULGC)

National Council of Teachers of Mathematics (NCTM)

National Educational Association (NEA)

National Music Publishers Association (NMPA)

National School Boards Association (NSBA)

National Science Teachers Association (NSTA)

National Video Resources (NVR)

Public Broadcasting System (PBS)

Recording Industry Association of America (RIAA)

Software Publishers Association (SPA)

Time Warner, Inc.

U.S. Copyright Office

U.S. National Endowment for the Arts (NEA)

Viacom, Inc.

6
Fair Use: Technology in the Library

- *Are there any guidelines for electronic reserves?*
- *What special requirements are there for duplicating sound works?*
- *Is making a duplicate in another tape format a violation of copyright?*

In this age of electronics, libraries are facing problems specific to the provision of services to their clientele. For school and college or university libraries, a big issue is that of electronic reserves.

Some general direction is given in guidelines developed by the American Library Association (ALA) in 1982 and revised in 1986.

LIBRARY RESERVE GUIDELINES

ALA's Library Reserve guidelines, part of the *ALA Model Policy Concerning College and University Photocopying for Classroom Research and Library Reserve Use*, allow a library—at the request of a faculty member—to photocopy and put on reserve excerpts from works in its collection "in accordance with guidelines similar to those governing formal classroom distribution for face-to-face teaching. . . . "[1] This statement has puzzled many people because the classroom guidelines don't seem to fit the reserve situation. For example, the very fact that material is on reserve to be shared by a number of students means that there is not likely to be a copy made for each student in the class. However, the statement may be there because ALA points out that the reserve shelf may function as an extension of classroom readings.

The library reserve section of the ALA policy includes the following provisos:

> In general, librarians may photocopy materials for reserve room use for the convenience of students both in preparing class assignments and in pursuing informal educational activities which higher education requires, such as advanced independent study and research.[2]

If the request calls for only one copy to be placed on reserve, the library may photocopy an entire article, or an entire chapter from a book, or an entire poem. Requests for multiple copies on reserve should meet the following guidelines:

1. the amount of material should be reasonable in relation to the total amount of material assigned for one term of a course taking into account the nature of the course, its subject matter and level, 17 U.S.C. §§107(1) and (3);
2. the number of copies should be reasonable in light of the number of students enrolled, the difficulty and timing of assignments, and the number of other courses which may assign the same material, 17 U.S.C. §107(1) and (3);
3. the material should contain a notice of copyright, see 17 U.S.C. §401;
4. the effect of photocopying the material should not be detrimental to the market for the work. (In general, the library should own at least one copy of the work.) 17 U.S.C. §107(4).[3]

For example, a professor may place on reserve as a supplement to the course textbook a reasonable number of copies of articles from academic journals or chapters from trade books. A reasonable number of copies will in most instances be less than six, but factors such as the length or difficulty of the assignment, the number of enrolled students and the length of time allowed for completion of the assignment may permit more in unusual circumstances.

In addition, a faculty member may also request that multiple copies of photocopied, copyrighted material be placed on reserve if there is insufficient time to obtain permission from the copyright owner. For example, a professor may place on reserve several photocopies of an entire article from a recent issue of *Time* magazine or the *New York Times* in lieu of distributing a copy to each member of the class. If you are in doubt as to whether a particular instance of photocopying is fair use in the reserve reading room, you should waive any fee for such a use.

ELECTRONIC RESERVES

Of those colleges and universities that have electronic reserve systems in place at this time, some have put their guidelines for electronic reserves on the Internet. An examination of these guidelines indicates that a number of resources are being consulted to help in their development. These resources include the document *Fair Use In the Electronic Age: Serving the Public Interest*, the *Electronic Reserve Listserv*, the *Copyright Listserv*, the *Model Policy concerning College and University Photocopying for Classroom, Research and Library Reserve Use*, and *Section 107 of the Copyright Law of the United States*.

Among the provisions included in electronic reserve policies, the most common are that the system must be available only to the particular institution's students, faculty, and staff; that documents placed on electronic reserve must carry a copyright warning; that certain materials such as lecture notes, student papers, exams, federal documents, one article from an issue of a serial, one chapter from a book, and items that are in the public domain are acceptable to the system; that access to any material is by course or professor name; and that copyrighted material placed on the system under the rubric of fair use must be erased at the end of each semester.

Since this is a developing area of copyright, those with an interest in electronic reserves must check all sources of information frequently. Currently, the Conference on Fair Use (CONFU) participants representing the American Association of Law Libraries, the American Council of Learned Societies, the Association of Academic Health Science Library Directors, the Association of American Universities, the Association of American University Presses, the Association of Research Libraries, the Indiana Partnership for Statewide Education, the Medical Library Association, the Music Library Association, the National School Board Association, and the special Libraries Association have generated draft guidelines for electronic reserves. These guidelines are entitled "Fair-Use Guidelines for Electronic Reserve Systems" and are now in the process of acquiring formal endorsements from the participating organizations. They are printed in their entirety in Appendix F.

SOUND RECORDINGS

The copyright law (Section 101) defines sound recordings as "works that result from the fixation of a series of musical, spoken, or other sounds, but not including the sounds accompanying a motion picture or other audiovisual work, regardless of the nature of the material objects, such as disks, tapes, or other phonorecords, in which they are embodied."

Phonorecords are then defined as "material objects in which sounds, other than those accompanying a motion picture or other audiovisual work, are fixed by any method now known or later developed, and from which the sounds can be perceived, reproduced, or otherwise communicated, either directly or with the aid of a machine or device. The term 'phonorecords' includes the material object in which the sounds are first fixed."

There are a number of reasons why educators and librarians in all types of libraries might wish to duplicate some types of sound recordings. First, for some formats, such as audiocassettes, copying can be done quickly with easily obtained and reasonably priced equipment. Disks can be copied by the very machine that plays them—the computer. Other technologies, such as CDs, are not easily copied as yet, but the day will undoubtedly come when that will no longer be true.

Second, some of the formats in which sound recordings are found are fairly fragile. Audiocassette tapes can break or be recorded over, and the plastic cases holding the tapes are subject to damage from both heat and cold. It may seem that the sensible thing to do is to save the original and make copies for users. That way, when something happens to a user copy, a new copy can be readily generated. *Don't do it!* There are no fair-use guidelines that have been agreed to specifically for sound recordings, so it is the law itself that must be used to address copying some or all of an audiocassette or other sound recording. Under fair use, it may be possible to copy a portion of an audiotape (or other type of phonorecording). But, if one applies the same rules to audiocassettes and other sound recordings as apply under the law to books and periodicals, it can be readily seen that copying the whole work is more likely than not to be an infringement. It is definitely not permissible to make copies of a whole book to meet a demand by students or library patrons, while keeping the original unused except for copying purposes. The same principle applies to sound recordings. (To facilitate a decision on whether or not to copy part or all of a sound recording, see the Fair Use Checklist, Table 6 in Chapter 4.)

A third reason that educators, researchers, and librarians might be tempted to copy a sound recording is to switch it from one medium to another. For example, if a library has some phonorecords in excellent condition in its collection, the more use they get, the greater the chance is that the quality will diminish. Wouldn't it be better to tape-record that phonorecord and let the tape be used instead? *No, it would not!* The change to another medium is an adaptation—one of the copyright holder's basic rights—and is an infringement.

The safe course of action is to buy the number of sound recordings that are needed, perhaps at a volume discount. Or, one might opt, of course, to obtain permission to use the material—whether for free or for a fee.

ENDNOTES

1. *Model Policy Concerning College and University Photocopying for Classroom Research and Library Reserve Use.* http://www.ala.org. Reprinted with permission of ALA.
2. Ibid.
3. Ibid.

7

Section 108: Special Privileges for Libraries and Archives

- *Do Section 108 privileges supersede the fair use doctrine?*
- *If a library makes a profit from photocopying, is it likely to lose the advantages of Section 108?*
- *What constitutes a "reasonable effort" to locate a replacement copy under Section 108?*
- *Does faxing create two copies of a work and thus violate Section 108?*

Part of the copyright law, Section 108, extends special privileges to qualifying libraries and archives. These privileges are of utmost importance to librarians and libraries, enabling them to better serve their patrons, including researchers, teachers, professors, and students. Entitled "Limitations on Exclusive Rights: Reproduction by Libraries and Archives," Section 108 allows libraries and archives that meet certain criteria to make and/or distribute copies of printed materials. Not only does this section make it possible for libraries to copy whole works for certain reasons, but it also allows copying for interlibrary loan to fill patron requests. And, of course, it is important to remember that Section 108 privileges coexist with the Section 107 fair use doctrine. One right does not preclude or cancel the other.

The law itself is relatively easy to read. Here we will look at each subsection of the law separately, with explanatory comments following each section.

Subsection (a)

The law states that

(a) Notwithstanding the provisions of section 106, it is not an infringement of copyright for a library or archives, or any of its employees acting within the scope of their employment, to reproduce no more than one copy or phonorecord of a work, or to distribute such copy or phonorecord, under the conditions specified by this section [of the law] if—

    (1) the reproduction or distribution is made without any purpose of direct or indirect commercial advantage:

    (2) the collections of the library or archives are

        (i) open to the public or

        (ii) available not only to researchers affiliated with the library or archives or with the institution of which it is a part, but also to other persons doing research in a specialized field; and

    (3) the reproduction or distribution of the work includes a notice of copyright.

While the language of the law is clear, the meaning of some of the words and phrases is less so. There are, however, a number of areas that can be interpreted with some certainty.

If fees are charged for copies, they should be on a cost-recovery basis to avoid running afoul of the stipulation that the reproduction or distribution must be made without any purpose of direct or indirect commercial advantage to the library or archives.

From the language of the law, the House Report (p. 75), and the Conference Report,[1] we know that a library in a for-profit organization is eligible for protection under Section 108, if the library is open to the public or available for research purposes to persons not affiliated with the organization, and if the reproduction and distribution is made without direct or indirect commercial advantage to the library. Through this mechanism, the collections of some special libraries are accessible to patrons who might not, otherwise, have the ability to obtain specialized materials. To date, there is an unanswered question: Must the collections of a library be open to persons unaffiliated with the institution doing specialized research or is availability through interlibrary loan enough? Translated, the question—for a library in a for-profit entity—becomes: To protect its Section 108 rights, must the library in a for-profit organization allow its competitors entry?

Section 106 is the part of the law that describes the bundle of rights that accrue to the copyright holder. These include the right to reproduce the work, the right to make derivative works, the right to sell or otherwise distribute the work, public performance rights, and public display rights.

According to Section 101 of U.S. copyright law, "copies" are material objects, other than phonorecords, in which a work is fixed by any method now known or later developed, and from which the work can be perceived, reproduced, or otherwise communicated, either directly or with the aid of a machine or device. The term copies includes the material object, other than a phonorecord, in which the work is first fixed.

The admonition that libraries may "reproduce no more than one copy" has come to mean that "libraries may reproduce no more than one copy at a time."

The requirement of placing a notice of copyright on the reproduced material was easily fulfilled when the copyright law of the United States mandated that to protect a copyright holder's rights, he or she must include certain information in a certain format. Since the United States joined the Berne Convention, there is no longer the former requirement for the copyright notice to be included on the verso of the title page with the abbreviation "copr." or the copyright symbol, followed by the year of publication and the name(s) of the copyright holder(s).

Subsection (b)

b)   The rights of reproduction and distribution under this section apply to a copy or phonorecord of an unpublished work duplicated in facsimile form solely for purposes of preservation and security or for deposit for research use in another library or archives of the type described by clause (2) of subsection (a), if the copy or phonorecord reproduced is currently in the collections of the library or archives.

This section of the law requires that the unpublished work be duplicated in "facsimile form." Webster's dictionary defines facsimile as "an exact copy or likeness." Microform reproduction is considered facsimile form.

While musical, pictorial, graphic, or sculptural works are not generally allowed to be copied under Section 108, it is interesting to note that unpublished works of *any type* are copyable under Section 108(b) for preservation and security purposes. The House Report 94–1476 (Judiciary Committee) of September 3, 1976, states that while this exemption is limited to unpublished works, it extends to any type of work, including photographs, motion pictures, and sound recordings. The report does not limit the type of copying to photocopying. The report says:

> Under this exemption, for example, a repository could make photocopies of manuscripts by microfilm or electrostatic process, but could not reproduce the work in "machine-readable" language for storage in an information system.

Obviously, this is an important statement in light of the technological capabilities available today, since it eliminates the possibility of electronic or digital storage.

Subsection (c)

(c)   The right of reproduction under this section applies to a copy or phonorecord of a published work duplicated in facsimile form solely for the purpose of replacement of a copy or phonorecord that is damaged, deteriorating, lost, or stolen, if the library or archives has, after a reasonable effort, determined that an unused replacement cannot be obtained at a fair price.

"Publication" is defined in Section 101 of the copyright law as

> the distribution of copies or phonorecords of a work to the public by sale or other transfer of ownership, or by rental, lease, or lending. The offering to distribute copies or phonorecords to a group of persons for purposes of further distribution, public performance, or public display, constitutes publication. A public performance or display of a work does not of itself constitute publication.

The House Report has some help for those wondering what constitutes a "reasonable effort" to locate a replacement copy for a deteriorating or stolen item in a library's collection. On that issue, the report says:

> The scope and nature of a reasonable investigation to determine that an unused replacement cannot be obtained will vary according to the circumstances of a particular situation. It will always require recourse to commonly-known trade sources in the United States, and in the normal situation also to the publisher or other copyright owner (if the owner can be located at the address listed in the copyright registration), or an authorized reproducing service.

It should be noted that it is an "unused replacement" for which this reasonable effort is allowed. Finding an unused replacement for older works may be difficult or impossible, especially in light of the fact that publishers no longer have federal tax-code support for retention of a stock of old titles. If one is found, it might have a rather high price tag, unless the title has been reprinted. If there is no unused copy available, the library or archives is allowed to reproduce the work.

The meaning of the phrase "fair price" is unclear, but factors affecting the price that must be considered include:

- original price
- age of the work
- condition (cover, binding, text block, paper, jacket)
- rarity
- whether the work is a classic in its field

Subsection (d)

(d) The rights of reproduction and distribution under this section apply to a copy, made from the collection of a library or archives where the user makes his or her request or from that of another library or archives, of no more than one article or other contribution to a copyrighted collection or periodical issue, or to a copy or phonorecord of a small part of any other copyrighted work, if—

    (1) the copy or phonorecord becomes the property of the user, and the library or archives has had no notice that the copy or phonorecord would be used for any purpose other than private study, scholarship, or research; and

    (2) the library or archives displays prominently, at the place where orders are accepted, and includes on its order form, a warning of copyright in accordance with requirements that the Register of Copyrights shall prescribe by regulation.

This portion of Section 108 sets limits on copying which may be lifted under certain conditions in subsection (e) below, so that these two portions of the guidelines—subsections (d) and (e)—should be looked at together.

This part of Section 108 allows a library to make one copy of an article from a periodical in its own collection, or to request from another library or archive one copy for a patron of something it does not own. If libraries commonly loaned whole issues of serials to requesting libraries, this section of the law would not have the importance that it has. However, for a number of reasons, including the fragility of paper copies, libraries owning serials prefer to make a copy of an article to send to the requesting library. This section of the guidelines, coupled with an expansion of patron rights in subsection (e) below, is of tremendous benefit to patrons.

The copyright warning, as developed by the Register of Copyrights, states:

> NOTICE: WARNING CONCERNING COPYRIGHT RESTRICTIONS
> The Copyright law of the U.S. (Title 17, United States Code) governs the making of photocopies or other reproductions of copyrighted material. Under certain conditions specified in the law, libraries and archives are authorized to furnish a photocopy or other reproduction. One of these specified conditions is that the photocopy or reproduction is not to be "used for any purpose other than private study, scholarship, or research." If a user makes a request for, or later uses, a photocopy or reproduction for purposes in excess of "fair use," that user may be liable for copyright infringement.
>
> This institution reserves the right to refuse to accept a copying order if, in its judgment, fulfillment of the order would involve violation of copyright law.

This notice must appear both at the place where orders for copying are taken and on the order form. When a patron is present at the point of ordering, then a paper copy of the request form with the warning imprinted is available for the patron to sign. Many requests for copies, however, are made off-site through the use of technology. This being the case, the mandate that the patron be made aware of the copyright warning has led many libraries to require that fax requests for copies and interlibrary loans be accepted only on a form that includes the warning. Online interlibrary loan systems may incorporate the warning as part of the on-screen request form. Telephone requests present a tough question—does reading the warning aloud suffice? Doubt that it is has led many libraries to send out their request form in response to telephone queries, slowing down the process but protecting the library's rights under Section 108.

Because a library may make only one copy for a patron there is a technological glitch in one form of document delivery that should be noted. Most fax machines in libraries today transmit only from single pages, that is, not from the journal or book but from a photocopy. That means that a document delivered via fax to a user leaves the library with a second copy on hand. The best course of action is to destroy that copy immediately after being assured that a readable copy has been received for the patron. One hopes that the next generation of fax machines will eliminate this problem.

If a library answers a patron request by scanning and sending the material electronically, a situation similar to the one involving fax machines arises. If the scanned copy is left on the computer, then a second copy exists, and that is a violation. The scan must be deleted.

Subsection (e)

(e) The rights of reproduction and distribution under this section apply to the entire work, or to a substantial part of it, made from the collection of a library or archives where the user makes his or her request or from that of another library or archives, if the library or archives has first determined, on the basis of a reasonable investigation, that a copy or phonorecord of the copyrighted work cannot be obtained at a fair price, if—

    (1) the copy or phonorecord becomes the property of the user, and the library or archives has had no notice that the copy or phonorecord would be used for any purpose other than private study, scholarship, or research; and

    (2) the library or archives displays prominently, at the place where orders are accepted, and includes on its order form, a warning of copyright in accordance with requirements that the Register of Copyrights shall prescribe by regulation.

The comments under subsection (d) above pertain to this portion of the law also, but subsection (e) expands patrons' rights. Libraries are authorized to copy an entire work, or a substantial part, under conditions that match those of subsection (d), but only if the library cannot find a copy for purchase at a fair price.

The unusual feature of this section is its allowance for expanded copying for a patron based on a library's failure to find and purchase a copy of a work for the user. The search for the work is not limited to an unused copy (see subsection (c) above for how the search must be conducted), perhaps making the job somewhat faster and easier. Also, there is the issue of fair price to be addressed (see subsection (c) above). And it is difficult to predict whether, in most instances, copying the work would be more time-consuming and expensive than searching for and buying the work for the patron. In order to avoid dealing with the problem, many libraries limit their copying to that allowed in subsection (d) above.

Subsection (f)

(f) Nothing in this section—

    (1) shall be construed to impose liability for copyright infringement upon a library or archives or its employees for the unsupervised use of reproducing equipment located on its premises: Provided, That such equipment displays a notice that the making of a copy may be subject to the copyright law:

    (2) excuses a person who uses such reproducing equipment or who requests a copy or phonorecord under subsection (d) from liability for copyright infringement for any such act, or for

any later use of such copy or phonorecord, if it exceeds fair use as provided by section 107;

(3) shall be construed to limit the reproduction and distribution by lending of a limited number of copies and excerpts by a library or archives of an audiovisual news program, subject to clauses (1),(2), and (3) of subsection (a); or

(4) in any way affects the right of fair use as provided by section 107, or any contractual obligations assumed at any time by the library or archives when it obtained a copy or phonorecord of a work in its collections.

This portion of the guidelines places the burden of responsibility for compliance with the copyright law on the library patron if the photocopier used by patrons is unsupervised *and* it displays a notice that making a copy may be subject to the copyright law.

Generally, unsupervised copiers are coin-operated machines. Many are not owned by the library but are owned and maintained by an outside vendor. "Unsupervised" does not mean that a staff member should refuse to give technical help to a patron who asks about how the material should be placed on the machine or how to make a darker copy. It does mean that staff should not do the copying or select what is to be copied.

Certainly, the Register of Copyright's warning (see subsection (d) above) would be considered adequate. It is, however, a fairly large notice—putting it on the equipment might be difficult.

While there have been suggestions for alternative notices by some groups, including the American Library Association, the safest course of action is to use the standard wording indicated in the law itself (see Appendix A).

When dealing with this area of patron use of copy machines, it is important to remember that the library or media center probably has several machines that copy items. Certainly, microform machines are in that category. Therefore, it makes sense to place the copyright notice on them. Libraries have public fax machines that transmit copies, too. Any machines that duplicate and that are used by the public would seem to require the placement of a warning regarding copyright.

Instructions for the use of each machine should be clearly posted on or near the equipment, so that the use by patrons is unsupervised. Not all of this kind of equipment will be coin-operated; therefore, staff will need to determine and collect such fees. That task should not be classified as supervision and will not negate the privileges of this section of the law.

Subsection (g)

(g) The rights of reproduction and distribution under this section extend to the isolated and unrelated reproduction or distribution of a single copy or phonorecord of the same material on separate occasions, but do not extend to cases where the library or archives, or its employee—

   (1) is aware or has substantial reason to believe that it is engaging in the related or concerted reproduction or distribution of multiple copies or phonorecords of the same material, whether made on one occasion or over a period of time, and whether intended for aggregate use by one or more individuals or for separate use by the individual members of a group;

   (2) engages in the systematic reproduction or distribution of single or multiple copies or phonorecords of material described in subsection (d): Provided, That nothing in this clause prevents a library or archives from participating in interlibrary arrangements that do not have, as their purpose or effect, that the library or archives receiving such copies or phonorecords for distribution does so in such aggregate quantities as to substitute for a subscription to or purchase of such work.

This portion of Section 108 has its own guidelines. The congressionally appointed National Commission on New Technological Uses of Copyrighted Works, in consultation with the major library, writer, and publisher associations, developed the following *Guidelines for the Proviso of Subsection 108(g)(2)*.

1. As used in the proviso of subsection 108(g)(2), the words " . . . such aggregate quantities as to substitute for a subscription to or purchase of such work" shall mean:

   (a) with respect to any given periodical (as opposed to any given issue of a periodical), filled requests of a library or archives (a "requesting entity") within any calendar year for a total of six or more copies of an article or articles published in such periodical within five years prior to the date of the request. These guidelines specifically shall not apply, directly or indirectly, to any request of a requesting entity for a copy or copies of an article or articles published in any issue of a periodical, the publication date of which is more than five years prior to the date when the request is made. These guidelines do not define the meaning, with respect to such a request, of " . . . such aggregate quantities as to substitute for a subscription to [such periodical]."

   (b) With respect to any other material described in subsection

108(d), (including fiction and poetry), filled requests of a requesting entity within any calendar year for a total of six or more copies or phonorecords of or from any given work (including a collective work) during the entire period when such material shall be protected by copyright.

2. In the event that a requesting entity:
    (a) shall have in force or shall have entered an order for a subscription to a periodical, or
    (b) has within its collection, or shall have entered an order for, a copy or phonorecord of any other copyrighted work, material from either category of which it desires to obtain by copy from another library or archives (the "supplying entity"), because the material to be copied is not reasonably available for use by the requesting entity itself, then the fulfillment of such request shall be treated as though the requesting entity made such copy from its own collection. A library or archives may request a copy or phonorecord from a supplying entity only under those circumstances where the requesting entity would have been able, under the other provisions of section 108, to supply such copy from materials in its own collection.

3. No request for a copy or phonorecord of any material to which these guidelines apply may be fulfilled by the supplying entity unless such request is accompanied by a representation by the requesting entity that the request was made in conformity with these guidelines.

4. The requesting entity shall maintain records of all requests made by it for copies or phonorecords of any materials to which these guidelines apply and shall maintain records of the fulfillment of such requests, which records shall be retained until the end of the third complete calendar year after the end of the calendar year in which the respective request shall have been made.

5. As part of the review provided for in subsection 108(i), these guidelines shall be reviewed not later than five years from the effective date of this bill.

Generally called the CONTU (Commission on New Technological Uses of Copyrighted Works) Guidelines, the *Guidelines for the Proviso of Subsection 108(g)(2)* were incorporated in the Conference Report on the Copyright Act of 1976 (see House Report 1733). These guidelines have been a safe-harbor standard for libraries engaged in borrowing from other libraries for last 20 years.

Sometimes called the CONTU rule of five, Section (1) allows a library or archive to obtain through interlibrary as many as five copies from a title (whether from the same issue or from a combination of issues) less than five years old, without seeking permission and without purchasing a subscription. Keep in mind that for serials the current five-year period changes with each new volume.

The CONTU rule of five does not apply to serials over five years old.

For a copyrighted work other than a periodical (including fiction and poetry), there is a limit of five instances of copying from it during a calendar year.

Section (4) puts the responsibility for keeping track of requests and fills on the requesting library.

While no one knows what the future holds regarding Section 108 rights, the National Information Infrastructure report points out that these guidelines were instituted when there were no "readily available systems for the supply of single copies of or for the licensing of the reproduction of multiple copies of copyrighted works."[2]

The report goes on to say that "a publisher's license to access or download all or a portion of the aggregated copyrighted works on a server might be viewed as the online equivalent of a subscription."[3]

Because of new technologies, the report asserts:

> A publisher might allow free access to a table of contents and then through an appropriate payment mechanism such as electronic cash or a credit card, license the downloading of a single article. This "publication on demand" might become an effective and economic substitute for interlibrary loan on the NII. While the precise nature of all such systems cannot be known at this time, it is clear that the CONTU Guidelines, while remaining effective for print materials, cannot readily be generalized to "borrowing" electronic publications.

While the availability of licensing arrangements continues to grow, librarians must keep in mind that this availability does not negate Section 108(g)(2). As the report goes on to say:

> While it is clear that Section 108 does not authorize unlimited reproduction of copies in digital form, it is equally clear that Section 108(g)(2) permits "borrowing" in electronic form for interlibrary loan in the NII environment, so long as such "borrowing" does not lead to "systematic" copying. However, the existence of such licensing systems in a world of electronic publishing may make it difficult, if not impossible, to define "subscription or purchase" as intended, and equally impossible to apply the existing guidelines to all electronic transactions.[4]

The Conference on Fair Use (see Chapter 4) is continuing its efforts to reach agreement on guidelines for this new technological era. If that effort fails, a regulatory or legislative solution may be needed. Changes are surely coming, but when, how, and what are still unanswered questions at this point. It is important that teachers, professors, researchers, and librarians be aware of what is being proposed and that they be vocal in their objections or support. Maintaining fair use and Section 108 rights are essential to the free exchange of ideas needed to assure an informed citizenry.

Subsection (h)

> (h) The rights of reproduction and distribution under this section do not apply to a musical work, a pictorial, graphic, or sculptural work, or a motion picture, or other audiovisual work other than an audiovisual work dealing with news, except that no such limitation shall apply with respect to rights granted by subsections (b) and (c), or with respect to pictorial or graphic works published as illustrations, diagrams, or similar adjuncts to works of which copies are reproduced or distributed in accordance with subsections (d) and (e).

Libraries are given the right under subsections (b) and (c) to copy all types of works—including musical, pictorial, graphic, sculptural, motion picture or audiovisual works—but only for their own collections. The copying must be for the purposes of preservation and security or for deposit for research use in another library or archives which qualifies for Section 108 protection.

For a user, subsection (h) makes it possible to copy illustrations, diagrams, charts, and similar items that are part of the article or portion of a work that is being copied.

House Report 94–1476 (p.32) says this about audiovisual news programs:

> . . . nothing in section 108 is intended to limit the reproduction and distribution by lending of a limited number of copies and excerpts of an audiovisual news program. This exemption is intended to apply to the daily newscasts of the national television networks, which report the major events of the day. It does not apply to documentary (except documentary programs involving news reporting as that term is used in section 107), magazine-format or other public affairs broadcasts dealing with subjects of general interest to the viewing public.

Clearly, then, taping of such programs as *60 Minutes, Primetime Live, Dateline NBC,* or *20/20* is not permitted. The news content of the nightly news, for example, is permitted.

Repeal of Subsection (i)

The original version of the law included a requirement for a review every five years, by the Register of Copyrights, to determine the extent to which section 108 achieved the intended statutory balancing of the rights of creators with the needs of users. That review requirement was repealed in 1992.

Until recently, libraries tended to be concerned mainly with the copying of printed materials. Now, of course, libraries are concerned as to the extent that Section 108 might allow for copying in a newer format, especially for interlibrary loan purposes—for example, putting a disk containing the requested information into a computer for transmission to a user. The copyright law, in Section 101, defines copies as "material objects, other than phonorecords, in which a work is fixed by any method now known or later developed. . . . " That being the case, Section 108 appears to allow copying of works in print or electronic formats.

There is, however, a general feeling of uncertainty and unease about the application of the law and the guidelines in the electronic environment in which libraries and archives are operating now. The expectation is that there will be more technology at higher sophistication and capability levels in the near future. One hopes that there will soon be guidelines, and perhaps needed changes in the law, to deal appropriately with the new technologies that are available to serve the public.

ENDNOTES

1. Conf. Rep. No. 1733, 94th Cong., 2d Sess. (1976).
2. NII report, 88–89.
3. Ibid.
4. Ibid, 89.

8
Contractual Agreements

- *What are some of the most important items to look for in a contract or licensing agreement?*
- *What distinguishes an exclusive license from a nonexclusive one?*
- *What is the best way to change a contract clause?*
- *Does a licensing agreement extinguish fair use rights?*

Contractual agreements represent a fast-growing phenomenon in the world of information. The subject tends to be something of a mystery for many who have suddenly been forced to deal with it. Since there is reason to believe that there will be an ever-increasing number of contractual agreements in the future, the topic is becoming one of increasing importance. For purposes of discussion here, *libraries* will be used to personify licensees and *publishers* to personify licensers.

The actual signatory for a library contract may be a representative of the parent institution—for example, in academic settings the president may be the only person able to make agreements for any portion of the college—but the library will be used here as the party to the contract. Publishers may have a similar situation—being a division of a giant corporation, for example, where only the home office can make agreements for the divisions—but they, too, will be considered the party to the contract here.

This chapter will attempt to clarify a number of aspects of contractual agreements—whether they are called contracts, licenses, agreements, or something else—as they affect the information resources that are already here and those to come.

There is little doubt, if one peruses the literature of the library and education worlds, that contractual agreements are increasing in number in direct relationship to the increasing number of electronic resources becoming available. This changing world of information provision is raising a plethora of questions—many of which are simply unanswerable at this time.

Perhaps the most important information that needs to be put forth on contractual agreements is that they are governed by state law. Because copyright is federal law, it is uniform in its application, nationwide. Such is not the case with contracts, however. Contract law can vary from state to state, which means that it is important to know something about the law of contracts in the library's state. It may also be important to know something about the contract law of the publisher's state, if it differs from that of the library. Such knowledge is particularly important in the case of an agreement that calls for the resolution of disputes to be decided under the laws of the state in which an out-of-state publisher is located.

Libraries of all types—academic, public, school, and special—are now involved in contractual agreements centered on resources that they make available to their publics. Usually, the type of agreement to which libraries are a party is a license.

LICENSES

There are exclusive and nonexclusive licenses. Exclusive licenses are those that transfer one or more of the copyright holder's rights to the licensee. These are not the type of licenses that libraries are generally involved with, although they can be.

Nonexclusive licenses are the type that libraries commonly hold. A nonexclusive license is one that allows the use, for a fee, of a copyright holder's work, with the copyright holder retaining all of the bundle of rights that accrue with the copyright. The license contains a series of clauses that are agreed to by the parties. Usually the contract is generated by the publisher and is delivered to the library for signing. This is generally the case since it is rare for a library to have the legal resources either to generate a contract or to negotiate with a publisher regarding individual contract clauses. Later in this chapter, there are tips on what to do and what to look at when presented with a fully formed contract.

Using a CD-ROM database containing an index to periodicals as an example, let us examine what to expect of a routine contractual agreement. Assume that a CD-ROM periodicals index is available, with hardware, on a school-year or 12-month basis. There is a contractual agreement available for either the school-year version or the 12-month version. The quoted price for each reflects the fact that more CDs are generated for the full-year version. In addition, a full-text version of each of these databases is available. The full-text versions have higher price tags, of course, than those that are simply indexes. New CDs are furnished each month (for only 10 months in the case of the school-year version). An addressed envelope is included with each new CD for the return to the publisher of previous month's CD, which is required by the agreement.

This seems like a pretty straightforward set of options. Is it? Let's examine how a license like this is generated and what kind of provisions it generally includes.

First, remember that contracts are negotiable—in whole or in part. Second, read every single word of a proposed contract. Third, if at all possible, seek the advice of a competent attorney before a library agrees to a contract.

The kinds of contracts or licenses that are common in libraries, like the one for the CD-ROM periodicals index, are generated by the legal counsel of the publisher. The job of their counsel is to protect the interests of the company. The contracts reflect that fact, as they should.

But who is looking out for the interests of the library? Often, the head librarian of a small public library is on his or her own on such matters, with some help from the library's board. A small college may not have an attorney on the staff. Schools systems normally don't have a copyright counsel. To reiterate, many libraries have no access to advice of counsel in matters of copyright. Even if legal advice is available, it's best that staff read the contract, noting the areas of concern. The terms of the agreement should be scrutinized carefully; in some instances they may need to be renegotiated.

To help with the process of reviewing the agreement, Table 8 outlines a few of the topics, with related questions, that may be useful as a basic checklist.

The particular agreement at issue must be carefully read, preferably by a number of staff members, and unacceptable terms should be noted. If legal counsel is available, the staff's objections to the language of the agreement should be forwarded to her or him for review.

Whether working alone or with the help of an attorney, librarians need to keep in mind the fact that contracts are negotiable instruments. Therefore, the library should attempt to change the terms that are not in their best interest. While this attempt may not work, nothing ventured is nothing gained. Though the publisher may not agree to all of the changes, there may at least be some improvement in the terms.

TABLE 8   Contract Checklist

1. *Length of Agreement*
    __ Annual?
    __ Multi-year with price break?
    __ Month-by-month?

2. *Price*
    What is the pricing based on?
    __ Is it user-based? If so, is the price based on peak use, rather than average use?
    __ Is it product-based (for example, 10 months of CDs versus 12 months)?
    __ Are longer-term contracts with lower prices available?

3. *Payment Schedule*
    __ Must the bill be paid before service begins or renews?
    __ Is there an annual fee?
    __ Are there monthly payments?
    __ Is the start/stop date of the contract appropriate for the library's fiscal year or should there be an adjustment?

4. *Venue*
    __ Under which state law does the contract propose that disputes be resolved? (This is very important, since there is a strong likelihood that the publisher and the library are in different states. Often, the publisher is relatively far away. Having to travel to or hire a lawyer in a distant state can be expensive and time-consuming.)
    __ Is there an arbitration clause? Who pays?

5. *Third-Party Damage*
    __ Does the contract make the library liable for third-party damage to the equipment or software? (The third party is the user. Should the library agree to be responsible for possible user damage of the equipment or software?)

6. *Repairs*
    __ Is technical assistance available over the phone or via e-mail to address minor problems that can be remedied by library staff with advice from publisher staff?

___With adjustment for time zones, when is this help available?

__ How are major repairs accomplished?

___What is the time-frame for repairs?

___Is there a fee—for some, or all types of repairs?

__ If repair doesn't work, what is the replacement policy?

___What is the time-frame for replacement?

___Is there an adjustment in billing or a refund for down time?

7. *Help*

__ Is there an 800 line for help with using the resource?

___Adjusting for time zones, what hours is this help available?

8. *Termination*

__ What are the provisions for termination of the agreement by the library?

___Are there penalties?

___What notice must be given?

__ What are the provisions for termination of the agreement by the publisher?

___Is there a refund?

9. *Users Group*

__ Is there a users group?

___When and where does it meet?

___What is its purpose?

10. *Confidentiality*

__ Is there a confidentiality clause that prevents the sharing of the terms of the contract with other libraries?

11. *Copying*

__ Is there some limitation on making copies of information contained on or in the resource?

Libraries that must handle the matter without professional help can alter contract clauses by striking out those parts that are unacceptable and inserting new ones. Initialing and dating the changes in the right margin next to each revision is the accepted practice. Once this work is completed, the document can be signed, with a notice typed in near the signature reading, "Subject to the terms indicated above."

One question that is often asked in workshops is "Will rights like fair use coexist with a contract?" The answer is, "It depends." The situation can be complicated. The Working Group report describes what can happen:

> Limitations on the exclusive rights, such as the first sale doctrine, fair use or library exemptions, may be overridden by contract. However, such contract terms can be enforced only under state law. For instance, the fair use of a work (outside the scope of the license) by a licensee whose license precludes any use other than that specified by the license would not be an infringement of copyright, but would be a breach of the license agreement. Licenses and other contracts cannot transform noninfringing uses (such as fair uses) into infringements; they can, however, make such uses violations of the terms and conditions of the agreements . . . [1]

This statement lends credence to the notion that contracts should be undertaken with the greatest care. Because people deal with a number of agreements in their personal lives, they get accustomed to simply signing on the dotted line. Not many people try to change the terms for a car loan, a mortgage, or a lease. It probably doesn't occur to the average individual that there is such a possibility. People often don't even bother to read the document, but rely, instead, on the brief explanation offered by the car salesman or bank employee or landlord. While each of these persons may be trying to be helpful, there is nothing as effective as reading the agreement for oneself.

When it comes to contracts between libraries and publishers, it is absolutely essential that the appropriate personnel read the proposed agreement, whether or not the company representative is willing to interpret the document.

Since licensing terms are a function of the marketplace—this is true in both personal or business situations—the ability to bargain these terms is dependent on a number of factors. If a library has legal counsel, that's an advantage. If it has a large budget and a need for a number of one publisher's products, that's an advantage. If the library is a member of a consortium that can bargain for improved terms and lower prices for its membership, that's an advantage. If the library belongs to a state organization that has developed or is developing a model contract that is fair to both libraries and publishers, that's an advantage. If the procedures of the library allow quick payment of bills, that's an advantage. Full, but fair, advantage should be taken of any strengths. Of course, since libraries need publishers and publishers need libraries, there is generally an interest on the part of both parties to work out a satisfactory agreement.

Sometimes, libraries may wish to initiate contracts. For example, copying not covered by fair use—videotapes and audiotapes—could become a contracted privilege. This kind of initiative may become routine as libraries become more familiar and comfortable with contractual agreements.

LICENSERS

Depending on the type of material involved, becoming a licensee may happen in a variety of ways. Dealing directly with the copyright holder is one method of obtaining permission for the use of material. However, in a number of instances, it is more likely that the person seeking to use a copyrighted work will deal with an organization whose purpose is to collect licensing fees for copyright holders.

The organization best known to librarians and educators is the Copyright Clearance Center (CCC) in Danvers, Massachusetts.[2] CCC, in business since 1978, is a nonprofit corporation sponsored by author and publisher organizations. Journal publishers from around the world register with CCC which then collects photocopy royalty fees from users on a per transaction basis, Transaction Reporting Service (TRS), or under a blanket license, Annual Authorization Service (AAS). AAS exists for the for-profit sector. There has not, thus far, been a similar service set up for nonprofit libraries or educational institutions, although CCC does handle the permissions requests of professors at colleges and universities whose bookstores belong to the National Association of College Stores. Academic libraries sometimes use TRS. At this time, CCC does not deal with electronic rights or copying. However, the licensing environment is changing so rapidly that CCC may institute such a service, if there is a clear need. Those who have an interest in that possibility, as well as in the services available presently, should contact CCC directly.

The ability to combine resources from a variety of formats into a multimedia program brings with it the need to seek permission via licensing from both the film and music industries. Both fields have had licensing organizations in place for many years. For example, the Motion Picture Licensing Corporation (MPLC)[3] provides annual blanket licenses that enable "home use only" videotapes or videodisks to be shown for public performance. With multimedia and motionmedia becoming more and more common in the educational setting, the film licensing agencies will necessarily become more familiar to those in the teaching and library professions.

The world of music has for years had organizations to oversee the collection of royalties for copyright holders. The best-known example is the American Society of Composers, Artists, and Publishers (ASCAP) which has for many years performed this service.

Interestingly, libraries and educational institutions are now becoming licensees to vendors for databases that consist of materials involving multiple licenses with publishers. One example of this is Ebscohost, which offers online full text to as many as 1,000 periodicals. Ebsco negotiates licenses with each of the publications it offers and then offers one license to its clients. Certainly, this is a much simpler arrangement for libraries than dealing individually with a host of periodicals publishers. Just as it makes sense to handle print periodicals subscriptions through a jobber, it also makes sense to get electronic subscriptions through a jobber.

Contracts in effect at this time and those that are to come will necessarily be of high interest to information providers and users alike. Resources available electronically are increasing in number and sophistication, while a publisher's ability to monitor use is also increasing. No license is so perfect that all the possibilities are covered.

For example, electronic formats present opportunities for new uses of copyrighted materials. These new uses are not necessarily anticipated in the contractual agreements that are generated presently. The issue of whether or not uses not specifically mentioned in a license are permitted is one that will undoubtedly result in interesting debate, if not in litigation.

Methods for licensing are also changing. The print contract may be replaced online. Collective licenses may be increasingly common. Licenses for a whole work might be replaced by fee-per-use agreements.[4] Educators will surely be seeking the permissions necessary for the creation of multimedia creations, an activity that may require different types of licenses for different media. Licenses dealing with computers are already common.

However, no matter what the subject of the contractual agreement is or how many agreements there are, library staff members must develop the skills needed to scrutinize contract terms. Even with the advent of computer programs that can check content and point out areas of concern, there is still a need for a thinking, knowledgeable person to make decisions about the appropriateness of the document's contents.

ENDNOTES

1. NII report, 50.
2. Copyright Clearance Center, 222 Rosewood Drive, Danvers, MA 01923; (508)750-8500.
3. Motion Picture Licensing Corporation, *Do You Show Home Videocassettes?* 1 (800) 462-8855.
4. NII report, 52.

Part III
Beyond Four Walls

9
Distance Learning, Technology, and Copyright

Q. What is distance learning and how is it accomplished?

A. In a distance learning situation, one or more students who are not in the physical presence of the teacher receive instruction through some method of technology.

The latest technology makes it possible for television monitors at the distance learning site to broadcast the picture and sound from a classroom where the teacher and on-site students are located. In the most sophisticated (and expensive) arrangements, monitors also allow for picture and sound transmission from the distance learning site back to the classroom. This means that there may be the equivalent of a face-to-face teaching situation.

However, there are a number of other, less-costly ways in which distance learning may be accomplished, including interaction between teacher and students via computer. Once the face-to-face teaching situation is not the model being used, different copyright issues emerge. The exemptions in the copyright law, and the guidelines developed for educational use of copyrighted materials, apply only to face-to-face teaching in a classroom setting.

Q. Would it be okay for the students receiving my course at a remote location to videotape the sessions for playback to those students who were absent on a given day?

A. Under copyright law, the copyright owner(s) would need to give written permission for such taping to occur. The faculty and the educational institution, as well as the copyright holders of materials transmitted, would need to allow the videotaping.

In addition, privacy rights can become an issue when students and others are videotaped in a classroom setting. Release forms giving videotaping and reuse permissions from students, faculty, and others present on camera are needed to avoid problems.

Q. I think I've developed a wonderful distance learning course— one that I've presented in my school system several times with great success. I'd like to package and sell it to other school systems. Can I do that?

A. It depends. There are a number of legal issues involved in the packaging-for-sale of courses such as the one you have developed. As far as the copyright law is concerned, you need to get written permission from all copyright holders, whether individuals or institutions, especially since the change in status from nonprofit to profit may affect fair use exemptions.

Releases from all parties would be important to avoid both privacy and copyright problems. A number of contract issues would be involved as well. Employing an attorney to attend to the myriad details of such a venture would be essential.

Q. Is there a part of the copyright law that I, as faculty, should be most familiar with when participating in distance learning situations?

A. While a general knowledge of the copyright law is important for everyone in the field of education, fair use is a doctrine that is generally very important for educators. In addition, Section 110 (see Appendix C for the text of Section 110)—particularly parts (1) and (2)—should be studied by those who get involved in distance education.

Q. Is it only publicly funded schools or colleges that are allowed to establish courses using distance learning?

A. Not at all. Private schools and colleges may make courses available using distance learning technology. Those that are nonprofit educational institutions have the same exemptions under the copyright law, assuming other conditions are met, that publicly funded educational entities have.

In fact, it is anticipated that businesses will conduct more and more training sessions using the technology that makes distance learning a reality today. Providing such training for business may become a business in itself. There are no exemptions, except perhaps that of fair use, under copyright for commercial uses of copyrighted materials.

Q. If the format of the distance education course being offered does not mimic a "real" classroom, what are the copyright implications?

A. Development of such a course should include a plan for obtaining permissions for use of copyrighted materials before the course begins. Copying and distribution rights must be sought. Substitute materials should be identified for instances where the fee for use is too high for the course budget or where permission is refused.

Q. Is copyright the only legal area into which distance education leads?

A. No. There is also the problem of transmission rights. While the copyright law, Section 110, provides an exemption for certain performances and displays, these are specific in nature. Section 110(2) states that the following activities do not infringe, under the conditions described:

> performance of a nondramatic literary or musical work or display of a work, by or in the course of a transmission, if—
>
> (A)   the performance or display is a regular part of the systematic instructional activities of a governmental body or a nonprofit educational institution, and
>
> (B)   the performance or display is directly related and of material assistance to the teaching content of the transmission, and
>
> (C)   the transmission is made primarily for—
>> (i)   reception in classrooms or similar places normally devoted to instruction, or
>> (ii) reception by persons to whom the transmission is directed because their disabilities or other special circumstances prevent their attendance in classrooms or similar places normally devoted to instruction, or
>> (iii) reception by officers or employees of governmental bodies as part of their official duties or employment. . . .

Under this portion of the law, it is quite possible that a distance education situation in which the technology used is that of interactive video might qualify as a face-to-face teaching situation. That issue has not been tested in the courts. The simpler, less costly methods of delivery, such as computer exchanges of information, do not seem to be covered by the law; thus they would require permission for use of copyrighted materials.

In any case, this section precludes the use of dramatic literary and musical works, a significant point for those involved in transmitting materials to learners in a location different from that of the instructor. In a face-to-face teaching situation, the law makes it possible, under specific circumstances, for a teacher to show a lawfully obtained videotape labeled for family viewing or one that has been taped off-the-air in the classroom. However, restrictions under Section 110(2) would prohibit the same materials from being transmitted to the distance education site. Only nondramatic materials, such as text, are transmittable under the present law.

Q. Are there guidelines that can be used when establishing distance education courses?

A. While copyright law is unsettled on most of the issues surrounding distance education, recently the Conference on Fair Use generated, and posted on the Internet, draft guidelines for "Distant Education." While these draft guidelines, reprinted in their entirety below, allow the transmission of copyrighted works to students enrolled in a distance learning course in a nonprofit educational institution, there are limitations that must be observed.

The draft guidelines apply only to the performance of a copyrighted work such as a dramatic work or an audiovisual work in only two distance education situations:

1. live interactive classes; or
2. recorded classes for later one-time transmission by the originating institution.

It is important that all educators involved with distance education programs closely monitor developments in this area.

CONFU GUIDELINES

I. Distant Learning
Educational Fair Use Guidelines For Distance Learning
Revised Draft
Phase I
October 30, 1996

1.1 Preamble
Fair use is a legal principle that provides certain limitations on the exclusive rights of copyright holders. The purpose of these guidelines is to provide guidance on the application of fair use principles by educators, scholars and students who use copyrighted works for distance education under fair use rather than by seeking authorization from the copyright owners for non-commerical purposes. The guidelines apply only to fair use in the context of copyright.

There is no simple test to determine what is fair use. Section 107 of the Copyright Act sets forth the four fair use factors which should be considered in each instance, based on the particular facts of a given case, to determine whether a use is a "fair use": (1) the purpose and character of the use, including whether use is of a commercial nature or is for non-profit educational purposes, (2) the nature of the copyrighted work, (3) the amount and substantiality of the portion used in relation to the copyrighted work as a whole, and (4) the effect of the use upon the potential market for or value of the copyrighted work.

While only the courts can authoritatively determine whether a particular use is a fair use, these guidelines represent the participants' consensus of conditions under which fair use should generally apply and examples of when permission is required. Uses that exceed these guidelines may or may not be fair use. The participants also agree that the more one exceeds these guidelines, the greater the use that fair use does not apply.

The limitations and conditions set forth in these guidelines do not apply to works in the public domain—such as works of the U.S. government or works on which the copyright has expired for which there are no copyright restrictions—or to works for which the institution has obtained permission for the particular use. Also, license agreements may govern the uses of some works and users should refer to the applicable license terms for guidance.

The participants who developed these guidelines met for an extended period of time and the result represents their collective understanding in this complex area. Because digital technology is in a dynamic phase, there may come a time when it is necessary to revise these guidelines. Nothing in these guidelines should be construed to apply to the fair use privilege in any context outside of educational and scholarly uses of distance education. The guidelines do not cover non-educational or commercial digitization or use at any time, even by nonprofit educational institutions. The guidelines are not intended to cover fair use of copyrighted works in other educational contexts such as educational multimedia projects, electronic reserves or digital images which may be addressed in other fair use guidelines.

This Preamble is an integral part of these guidelines and should be included whenever the guidelines are reprinted or adopted by organizations and educational institutions. Users are encouraged to reproduce and distribute these guidelines freely without permission; no copyright protection of these guidelines is claimed by any person or entity.

1.2 Background

Section 106 of the Copyright Act defines the right to perform or display a work as an exclusive right of the copyright holder. The Act also provides, however, some exceptions under which it is not necessary to ask the copyright holders permission to perform or display a work. One is the fair use exception contained in section 107, which is summarized in the preamble. Another set of exceptions, contained in sections 110(1)–(2), permit instructors and students to perform or display copyright materials without permission from the copyright holder under certain carefully defined conditions.

Section 110(1) permits teachers and students in a nonprofit educational institution to perform or display any copyrighted work in the course of face-to-face teaching activities. In face-to-face instruction, such teachers and students may act out a play, read aloud a poem, display a cartoon or a slide, or play a videotape so long as the copy of the videotape was lawfully obtained. In essence, section 110(1) permits performance and display of any kind of copyrighted work, and even a complete work, as a part of face-to-face instruction.

Section 110(2) permits performance of a nondramatic literary or musical work or display of any work as a part of a transmission in some distance learning contexts, under the specific conditions set out in that section. Section 110(2) does not permit performance of dramatic or audiovisual works as a part of a transmission. The statute further requires that the transmission be directly related and of material assistance to the teaching content of the transmission and that the transmission be received in a classroom or other place normally devoted to instruction or by persons whose disabilities or special circumstances prevent attendance at a classroom or other place normally devoted to instruction.

The purpose of these guidelines is to provide guidance for the performance and display of copyrighted works in some of the distance learning environments that have developed since the enactment of section 110 and that may not meet the specific conditions of section 110(2). They permit instructors who meet the conditions of these guidelines to perform and display copyrighted works as if they were engaged in face-to-face instruction. They may, for example, perform an audiovisual work, even a complete one, in a one-time transmission to students so long as they meet the other conditions of these guidelines. They may not, however, allow such transmissions to result in copies for students unless they have permission to do so, any more than face-to-face instructors may make copies of audio-visual works for their students without permission.

The developers of these guidelines agree that these guidelines reflect the principles of fair use in combination with the specific provisions of sections 110(1)–(2). In most respects, they expand the provisions of section 110(2).

In some cases students and teachers in distance learning situations may want to perform and display only small portions of copyrighted works that may be permissible under the fair use doctrine even in the absence of these guidelines. Given the specific limitations set out in section 110(2), however, the participants believe that there may be a higher burden of demonstrating that fair use under section 107 permits performance or display of more than a small portion of a copyrighted work under circumstances not specifically authorized by section 110(2).

1.3 Distance Learning in General

Broadly viewed, distance learning is an educational process that occurs when instruction is delivered to students physically remote from the location or campus of program origin, the main campus, or the primary resources that support instruction. In this process, the requirements for a course or program may be completed through remote communications with instructional and support staff including either one-way or two-way written, electronic or other media forms.

Distance education involves teaching through the use of telecommunications technologies to transmit and receive various materials through voice, video and data. These avenues of teaching often constitute instruction on a closed system limited to students who are pursuing educational opportunities as part of a systematic teaching activity or curriculum and are officially enrolled in the course. Examples of such analog and digital technologies include telecourses, audio and video teleconferences, closed broadcast and cable television systems, microwave and ITFS, compressed and full-motion video, fiber optic networks, audiographic systems, interactive videodisk, satellite-based and computer networks.

2. APPLICABILITY AND ELIGIBILITY

2.1 APPLICABILITY OF THE GUIDELINES

These guidelines apply to the performance of lawfully acquired copyrighted works not included under section 110(2) (such as a dramatic work or an audiovisual work) as well as to uses not covered for works that are included in section 110(2). The covered uses are (1) live interactive distance learning classes (i.e., a teacher in a live class with all or some of the students at remote locations) and (2) faculty instruction recorded without students present for later transmission. They apply to delivery via satellite, closed circuit television or a secure computer network. They do not permit circumventing anti-copying mechanisms embedded in copyrighted works.

These guidelines do not cover asynchronous delivery of distance learning over a computer network, even one that is secure and capable of limiting access to students enrolled in the course through PIN or other identification system. Although the participants believe fair use of copyrighted works applies in some aspects of such instruction, they did not develop fair use guidelines to cover these situations because the area is so unsettled. The technology is rapidly developing, educational institutions are just beginning to experiment with these courses, and publishers and other creators of copyrighted works are in the early stages of developing materials and experimenting with marketing strategies for computer network delivery of distance learning materials. Thus, consideration of whether fair use guidelines are needed for asynchronous computer network delivery of distance learning courses perhaps should be revisited in three to five years.

In some cases, the guidelines do not apply to specific materials because no permission is required, either because the material to be performed or displayed is in the public domain, or because the instructor or the institution controls all relevant copyrights. In other cases, the guidelines do not apply because the copyrighted material is already subject to a specific agreement. For example, if the material was obtained pursuant to a license, the terms of the license apply. If the institution has received permission to use copyrighted material specifically for distance learning, the terms of that permission apply.

2.2   ELIGIBILITY

2.2.1   ELIGIBLE EDUCATIONAL INSTITUTION: These guidelines apply to nonprofit of educational institutions at all levels of instruction whose primary focus is supporting research and instructional activities of educators and students but only to their nonprofit activities. They also apply to government agencies that offer instruction to their employees.

2.2.2   ELIGIBLE STUDENTS: Only students officially enrolled for the course at an eligible institution may view the transmission that contains works covered by these guidelines. This may include students enrolled in the course who are currently matriculated at another eligible institution. These guidelines are also applicable to government agency employees who take the course or program offered by the agency as a part of their official duties.

3.   WORKS PERFORMED FOR INSTRUCTION

3.1   RELATION TO INSTRUCTION: Works performed must be integrated into the course, must be part of systematic instruction and must be directly related and of material assistance to the teaching content of the transmission. The performance may not be for entertainment purposes.

4.   TRANSMISSION AND RECEPTION

4.1   TRANSMISSION (DELIVERY): Transmission must be over a secure system with technological limitations on access to the class or program such as a PIN number, password, smartcard or other means of identification of the eligible student.

4.2   RECEPTION: Reception must be in a classroom or other similar place normally devoted to instruction or any other site where the reception can be controlled by the eligible institution. In all such locations, the institution must have in place the technological means to prevent copying of the portion of the class session that contains performance of the copyrighted work.

5.   LIMITATIONS:

5.1   ONE TIME USE: Performance of an entire copyrighted work or a large portion thereof may be transmitted only once for a distance learning course. For subsequent performances, displays or access, permission must be obtained.

5.2   REPRODUCTION AND ACCESS TO COPIES

5.2.1   RECEIVING INSTITUTION: The institution receiving the transmission may record or copy classes that include the performance of an entire copyrighted work, or a large portion thereof, and retain the recording or copy for up to 15 consecutive class days (i.e., days in which the institution is open for regular instruction) for viewing by students enrolled in the course. Access to the recording or copy for such viewing must be in a controlled environment such as a classroom, library or media center, and the institution must prevent copying by students of the portion of the class session that contains the performance of the copyrighted work. If the institution wants to retain the recording or copy of the transmission for a longer period of time, it must obtain permission from the rightsholder or delete the portion which contains the performance or the copyrighted work.

5.2.2   TRANSMITTING INSTITUTION: The transmitting institution may, under the same terms, reproduce and provide access to copies of the transmission containing the performance of a copyrighted work; in addition, it can exercise reproduction rights provided in section 112(b).

6.   MULTIMEDIA

6.1   COMMERCIALLY PRODUCED MULTIMEDIA: If the copyrighted multimedia work was obtained pursuant to a license agreement, the terms of the license apply. If, however, there is no license, the performance of the copyrighted elements of the multimedia works may be transmitted in accordance with the provisions of these guidelines.

7.   EXAMPLES OF WHEN PERMISSION IS REQUIRED:

7.1   Commercial uses: Any commercial use including the situation where a nonprofit educational institution is conducting courses for a for-profit corporation for a fee such as supervisory training courses or safety training for the corporations employees.

7.2 Dissemination of recorded courses: An institution offering instruction via distance learning under these guidelines wants to further disseminate the recordings of the course or portions that contain performance of a copyrighted work.

7.3 Uncontrolled access to classes: An institution (agency) wants to offer a course or program that contains the performance of copyrighted works to non-employees.

7.4 Use beyond the 15-day limitation: An institution wishes to retain the recorded or copied class session that contains the performance of a copyrighted work not covered in section 110(2). (It also could delete the portion of the recorded class session that contains the performance).

ENDORSING ORGANIZATIONS:

Organizations Participating in Developing but not Necessarily Endorsing or Supporting These Guidelines:

American Association of Community Colleges
American Association of Law Libraries
American Council of Learned Societies
Association of American Publishers
Association of American Universities
Association of College and Research Libraries
Association of Research Libraries
Broadcast Music, Inc.
City University of New York
Coalition of College and University Media Centers
Creative Incentive Coalition
Houghton Mifflin
Indiana Partnership
John Wiley & Sons, Inc.
Kent State University
National Association of State Universities and Land Grant Colleges
National Geographic
National School Board Association
Special Libraries Association
State University of New York
U.S. Copyright Office
University of Texas System
Utah State University
Viacom

10

The Worldwide View

- *Is there such a thing as an international copyright law that applies to every country in the world?*
- *How should material copyrighted outside the United States be treated?*
- *Will the restoration of copyright to some items formerly in the public domain adversely affect the activities of educators, librarians, and researchers?*
- *How do the moral rights of visual artists affect libraries and educational institutions?*

National copyright laws apply only within their own country. To extend copyright protection, countries must enter into agreements with other nations. Some of these agreements are between individual countries (bilateral); more common are agreements between many countries (multilateral). An agreement may not require a signatory to make changes in its existing copyright laws. In other cases, the agreement may set standards that must be met before a country is able to sign it.

In this chapter we will look at how these international agreements affect the work of libraries and educational institutions. In particular, we will look at how works copyrighted outside the United States should be handled. In addition we will look at two important changes that international agreements have made on U.S. copyright law—the moral rights of visual artists and the restoration of copyright to some works formerly in the public domain—and see how educators, librarians, and researchers should deal with these.

INTERNATIONAL COPYRIGHT AGREEMENTS

Bilateral Agreements

The United States did not protect the rights of foreign authors until Congress passed the Chace Act in 1891.[1] Prior to that, anyone in the United States was free to copy foreign works without violating any U.S. copyright laws. The reluctance to respect the copyrights of authors outside the United States was purely economic. The United States imported considerably more copyrighted works than it exported. The United States had little to lose economically if other countries refused to accord U.S. works any copyright protection.

World War II exposed the world to American movies, books, magazines, and other copyrighted materials. As exports of copyrighted materials increased, the United States began to move toward making U.S. copyright laws more compatible with the countries they traded with. Pirating in these countries resulted in lost revenue for American industries. "The U.S. International Trade Commission estimated recently that U.S. companies lost between $43 billion and $61 billion during 1986 because of inadequate legal protection for United States intellectual property, including copyrights."[2]

The first steps the United States took toward international protection of works by American authors was to conclude bilateral agreements with major countries such as England, France, Germany, and Italy. These agreements essentially guaranteed that each country would treat the works of the others' authors as it does its own.

The Universal Copyright Convention

As American trade increased, it became apparent that bilateral arrangements could not accomplish the task. Too many countries were still free to pirate American works. The problem for the United States was that the principal multilateral copyright agreement in the world, the Berne Union for the Protection of Literary and Artistic Property (Berne Convention), required significant changes in U.S. copyright law and this would take time. For example, a major sticking point was the manufacturing clause[3] which was designed to protect American printers from foreign competition. The clause required books and periodicals in the English language to be printed in the United States or Canada to receive full copyright protection. The printing industry needed more time to become more competitive with international competition. The manufacturing clause was repealed in 1976 but through extensions it remained in effect up to July 1, 1986.[4]

The problem remained to find a way for the United States to join a multilateral copyright agreement and not have to make significant changes in its own laws. The only answer seemed to be to create a new multilateral agreement that would not require changes in U.S. law.

This agreement was called the Universal Copyright Convention of 1952 (UCC). The United States became a founding member of UCC, which went into force in the United States on September 16, 1955. In general, works copyrighted in UCC countries were treated in the U.S. as if they had completed all the formalities required by the U.S. copyright law. It remains in effect and has over 80 countries as members. UCC is administered by the United Nations Educational Scientific and Cultural Organization (UNESCO).

For the United States the principal weakness of UCC, however, proved to be the same as the reason it was founded. Under UCC, member countries are not required to raise their standards. They are also only obligated to protect to the level they provide to their own citizens. If a member did not adequately protect its own citizens, it therefore followed that it would not protect the rights of other UCC countries within its borders.

Berne Convention

It became clear that the United States had to become a member of the Berne Convention in order to protect its own economic interests. Both UCC and Berne require their members to accord to the nationals of other member countries the same level of copyright protection that they provide to their own citizens. Signatories of the Berne Convention, however, must adhere to a certain minimal level of protection for their own citizens before being allowed to sign. This requirement guarantees that each member country is assured of certain basic protections. The Berne Convention of 1886 is the oldest international copyright agreement. It is also the largest multilateral agreement governing international copyright in the world today.

The U.S. joined the Berne Convention not only because it offered the highest available level of copyright protection available, but also because Berne offered

- Additional rights. In addition to the general rights available under UCC, members of the Berne Convention are guaranteed duration of copyright for life of the author plus 50 years, and rights of translation, reproduction, public performance, broadcasting, adaptation, and arrangement.
- More countries. The United States immediately gained copyright relations with 24 countries with which it had no current relations.
- International policy. U.S. membership in the Berne Convention also makes it possible for the United States to participate in the formulation and management of international copyright policy.[5]

In short, membership in the Berne Convention was clearly in the national interest because it ensures a "strong, credible U.S. presence in the global marketplace."[6]

Trade-Related Aspects of Intellectual Property

As part of the General Agreement on Tariffs and Trades (GATT), the Uruguay Round was concluded on December 15, 1993. On December 8, 1994, President Clinton signed the Uruguay Round Agreements Act (URAA) which implements the Uruguay Round Agreement on Tariffs and Trade. Title V includes an agreement on the Trade-Related Aspects of Intellectual Property (TRIPS).[7]

In addition, the GATT agreement discussed in Chapter 2 now allows the United States to use trade sanctions to enforce international copyright agreements.

Implications

For educators, librarians, and researchers international copyright agreement means

- There is no such thing as an international copyright law that governs all nations.
- Copyrights of other countries generally do not have any effect in the United States unless the United States has signed a bilateral agreement with that country or that country is a member of a multilateral copyright agreement that the United States has signed.[8]
- Signatories of copyright conventions or treaties generally only receive the same copyright protection that another member country provides to its own citizens.
- It is not necessary to know the copyright law of another country. One need only understand U.S. copyright law. Foreign copyrighted works are treated in the United States the same as works copyrighted in the United States.

This means that there are two options when it comes to copying, performing, or publicly displaying works that are copyrighted in a foreign country but not in the United States:

1. determine if the work is protected under the U.S. copyright law; or
2. treat a foreign work just as you would any work copyrighted in the United States

To determine if a foreign work is covered involves some investigation. First, it is necessary to determine if the foreign country has or is part of an international copyright agreement to which the United States is a signatory. Second, determine when that country became a signatory since international copyright agreements are usually not retroactive.[9]

The second method is to treat the work as if it were copyrighted in the United States. This method is a good practice unless you know for sure that a foreign copyrighted work is not protected in the United States.

RESTORATION OF COPYRIGHTS

The Uruguay Round Agreements Act[10] contained provisions for the restoration of copyright protection to works already in the public domain in the United States but still under protection in the WTO or Berne member country that was the source of the work.[11] At first, this would seem to pose a very difficult problem. It is possible that a work[12] that could be freely copied today because it is in the public domain could not be copied tomorrow because it is suddenly protected by copyright.

Educators, librarians, and researchers should understand that:

- Restoration will most affect publishers who are still marketing restored work and authors who have created a derivative version such as a dramatization.
- The titles of the works that will be restored can be easily learned.[13]
- Restoration requires notice and ample time to correct. [14]

Under procedures in the act, copyright restoration is automatic but copyright owners must file a notice of intent to enforce (NIE) their restored copyright. One year after the notice is published in the *Federal Register*[15] and/or properly served on someone who would be infringing at the end of the year if that person (called the reliance party) continued, the copyright owner can enforce the copyright. Reliance parties, therefore, have one year to desist, sell off their stock, or reach an agreement with the copyright owner.[16] Above all, the same limitations placed on all copyright owners— first sale, no copyright to the facts and ideas in the work, and fair use—still apply to restored works.

MORAL RIGHTS IN COPYRIGHT

One of the principal obstacles to the United States signing the Berne Convention was the recognition of moral rights. In 1990 Congress passed the Visual Rights Act[17] which gave the artists the rights of attribution and integrity. Attribution "ensures that artists are correctly identified with the works of art they create, and that they are not identified with works created by others."[18] Integrity "allows artists to protect their works against modification and destructions that are prejudicial to their honor or reputation."[19] These rights are close to those articulated in Article 6*bis*[20] of the Berne Convention.

Prior to the 1990 act, 11 states (California, Connecticut, Illinois, Louisiana, Maine, Massachusetts, New Jersey, New Mexico, New York, Pennsylvania, and Rhode Island) had enacted artists' rights laws. The first bill to protect visual artists was introduced in Congress in 1979, the same year that California passed its Art Preservation Act. Even today some state statutes offer greater protection than the federal law.

As the owners of works of art, including works that are part of library and school buildings, it is important for educators and librarians to understand the moral rights of artists under both federal and state law. In particular, they should be aware that

- Changes in a work of art that are the result of time or the natural aging of the material of which it is made are not covered by the act.[21]
- Changes made to the work that are the result of conservation or of public presentation (lighting or placement, for example) are excluded unless they are the result of gross negligence.[22]
- The act does not apply to any "reproduction, depiction, portrayal or other use. . . ."[23]
- The artist's rights under this act can be waived if the artist agrees to a waiver in a written instrument.[24]

The act only applies to "intentional distortion, mutilation."[25] Unlike other areas of copyright, it is also important to check your state laws.

ENDNOTES

1. 26 Stat. 1106, ch. 565.
2. Senate Report (Judiciary Committee) No. 100–352, May 20, 1988 (to accompany S. 1301), 2.
3. 17 U.S.C. § 601. Its roots go back to the Statute of Henry VII (1534), 25 Henry 8, chap. 15.
4. The clause was set to expire on July 1, 1982, but the deadline was extended to July 1, 1986. Pub. L. No. 97–215 (July 13, 1982).
5. These reasons are set forth in Senate Report (Judicial Committee) No. 100–352, May 20, 1988 (to accompany S.1301), 2–4.
6. Senate Report (Judiciary Committee) No. 100–352, May 20, 1988 (to accompany S. 1301), 2.
7. Uruguay Round Agreements Act, Pub. L. No. 103–465 (October 18, 1994).
8. There are also some other additions: unpublished works are covered no matter what the nationality or domicile of the author; works first published by the U.N. or O.A.S.; works which come within the scope of a Presidential Proclamation. See 17 U.S.C. §104.
9. For a country-by-country listing see *U.S. Copyright Office Circular 38a*, "International Copyright Relations of the United States."
10. Uruguay Round Agreements Act, Pub. L. No. 103–465 (October 18, 1994).
11. According to 17 U.S.C. 104A(h)(6), to qualify for restoration, a work must be an original work of authorship that is not in the public domain in its source country through expiration of term of protection but is in the public domain in the United States due to (1) noncompliance with formalities imposed at any time by United States copyright law, including failure of renewal, lack of proper notice, or failure to comply with any manufacturing requirements; (2) lack of subject matter protection in the case of sound recordings fixed before February 15, 1972; or (3) lack of national eligibility. In addition, (1) at least one author or copyright owner had to have been, at the time the work was created, a national or domiciliary of an eligible country, and (2) if published, was first published in an eligible country and not published in the United States during the 30-day period following publication in such eligible country.
12. A work meeting these requirements is protected "for the remainder of the term of copyright that the work would have otherwise been granted in the United States if the work never entered the public domain in the United States."
    17 U.S.C. 104A(a)(1)(B).
13. The lists identifying restored works and their owners are available for public inspection in the Public Information Office of the U.S. Copyright Office, Library of Congress, Room 401, James Madison Building, 101 Independence Avenue, S.E., Washington, DC. Additionally, the images of the complete NIEs are available for inspection and copy-

ing in the Copyright Office Card Catalog, LM-459. Records of these NIEs have been indexed by the English title, the foreign title, the name of the author, and the name of the copyright owner. These records are available both online in the Copyright Office and via the Internet. Internet site addresses are http://lcweb.loc.gov/copyright (World Wide Web), marvel.loc.gov (gopher), and locis.loc.gov (telnet). The Copyright Office will perform a search of these records upon the receipt of a written request and the statutory search fee of $20 per hour or fraction thereof. For a fee, the Copyright Office will also make copies of NIEs or the list identifying restored works and their owners listed alphabetically by copyright owner; multiple works owned by a particular copyright owner are listed alphabetically by title.

14. 17 U.S.C. §104A.
15. According to U.S.C. 104A(e)(1)(B), the Register of Copyrights will publish in the *Federal Register*, not later than four months after the date of restoration for a particular nation and every four months thereafter for a period of two years, lists identifying restored works and the ownership thereof if a notice of intent to enforce a restored copyright has been filed. The first list was published May 1, 1996.
16. According to 17 U.S.C. 104A(d)(2) a reliance party can continue to use a restored copyright which it acquired before the date of enactment of the URAA, December 8, 1994, for a 12-month period beginning on the date of publication of the list identifying the restored work in the *Federal Register*.
17. Pub. L. No. 101–650, 104 Stat. 5128, 5133 (December 1, 1990).
18. House Report (Judiciary Committee) No. 101–514, June 1, 1990 (to accompany H.R. 2690), 5.
19. Ibid.
20. Article 6*bis* (1) states that

   Independently of the author's economic rights, and even after the transfer of the said rights, the author shall have the right to claim authorship of the work and to object to any distortion, mutilation or other modification of, or other derogatory action in relation to, the said work, which would be prejudicial to his honor or reputation

21. 17 U.S.C. 106A subsection c(1).
22. 17 U.S.C. 106A subsection c(2).
23. 17 U.S.C. 106A subsection c(3).
24. 17 U.S.C. 106A subsection e(1).
25. 17 U.S.C. 106A subsection a(3)(A).

Glossary of Terms Related to Copyright

Anonymous work—a work on which no person or other entity is identified as author.

Anthology—see *Collective work* and *Compilation*.

Architectural work—the design of a building as embodied in any tangible medium of expression, including a building, architectural plans, or drawings. Includes the overall form as well as the arrangement and composition of spaces and elements in the design, but does not include individual standard features.

Archival copies—backup copies of computer software which are to be used in case of failure of the originals. In cases where a copy is placed on the hard drive of a computer, the originals function as archival copies.

Author—the creator of a work; or the enterprise that employs a creator of a work made in the course of that employment; or an entity that commissions a work for hire.

Berne Convention—the Convention for the Protection of Literary and Artistic Works, signed at Berne, Switzerland, on September 9, 1886, and all acts, protocols, and revisions thereto.

Berne Convention work—a work is a "Berne Convention work" if

1. in the case of an unpublished work, one or more of the authors is a national of a nation adhering to the Berne Convention, or in the case of a published work, one or more of the authors is a national of a

nation adhering to the Berne Convention on the date of first publication;

2. the work was first published in a nation adhering to the Berne Convention, or was simultaneously first published in a nation adhering to the Berne Convention and in a foreign nation that does not adhere to the Berne Convention;

3. in the case of an audiovisual work—
   a. if one or more of the authors is a legal entity, that author has its headquarters in a nation adhering to the Berne Convention; or
   b. if one or more of the authors is an individual, that author is domiciled, or has his or her habitual residence in a nation adhering to the Berne Convention; or

4. in the case of a pictorial, graphic, or sculptural work that is incorporated in a building or other structure, the building or structure is located in a nation adhering to the Berne Convention; or

5. in the case of an architectural work embodied in a building, such building is erected in a country adhering to the Berne Convention.

For purposes of paragraph 1, an author who is domiciled in or has his or her habitual residence in a nation adhering to the Berne Convention is considered to be a national of that nation. For purposes of paragraph 2, a work is considered to have been simultaneously published in two or more nations if its dates of publication are within 30 days of one another.

Best edition—the edition, published in the United States at any time before the date of deposit, that the Library of Congress determines to be most suitable for its purposes.

Certificate of registration—as a validation of a copyright, this certificate demonstrates that the Copyright office approved the applicant's copyright application by stamping it with a registration number, date, and the Copyright office seal.

Coauthors—see *Joint work*.

Collective work—a work, such as a periodical issue, anthology, or encyclopedia, in which a number of contributions, constituting separate and independent works in themselves, are assembled into a collective whole.

Common law copyright—an author's right to his or her own work which is believed to have existed before there was a written statute.

Compilation—a work formed by the collection and assembling of preexisting materials or of data that are selected, coordinated, or arranged in such a way that the resulting work as a whole constitutes an original work of authorship. This term includes collective works.

Computer program—a set of statements or instructions to be used directly or indirectly in a computer in order to bring about a certain result.

CONFU (Conference on Fair Use)—a group of librarians, educators, publishers, and other interested parties who are working on guidelines for copyright use in the network environment of the National Information Infrastructure.

Copies—material objects, other than phonorecords, in which a work is fixed by any method now known or later developed, and from which the work can be perceived, reproduced, or otherwise communicated, either directly or with the aid of a machine or device. This term includes the material object, other than a phonorecord, in which the work is first fixed.

Copyright—the bundle of rights that accrue to a copyright holder. See Section 106 in Appendix B for details.

Copyright owner—with respect to any one of the exclusive rights comprising a copyright (see Section 106 in Appendix B), refers to the owner of that particular right.

Creation—fixation of a work in a copy or phonorecord for the first time; where a work is prepared over a period of time, the portion of it that has been fixed at any particular time constitutes the work as of that time, and where the work has been prepared in different versions, each version constitutes a separate work.

Deposit copies—an applicant for a copyright must make a deposit of copies or other representation of a work, such as photographs, to the Copyright office. Some formats require two such copies, while others only require one.

Derivative work—a work based on one or more preexisting works, such as a translation, musical arrangement, dramatization, fictionalization, motion picture version, sound recording, art reproduction, abridgment, condensation, or any other form in which a work may be recast, transformed, or adapted. A work consisting of editorial revisions, annotations, elaborations, or other modifications which, as a whole, represent an original work of authorship, is a "derivative work."

Device, machine, or process—for purposes of the copyright law, one now known or later developed.

Display—to show a copy of a work, either directly or by means of a film, slide, television image, or any other device or process or, in the case of a motion picture or other audiovisual work, to show individual images nonsequentially.

Duration—the duration of a copyright is dependent on the date of creation. For those works created on January 1, 1978, or later, the copyright lasts

1. for a sole author—life of the author plus 50 years;
2. for joint authors—life of the longest living author plus 50 years;
3. for works for hire, anonymous, or pseudonymous works—75 years from publication or 100 years from creation, whichever comes first.

For those works created or published before January 1, 1978, the copyright lasts

1. for published works—75 years from the date of publication, if renewal requirements were followed
2. for works that remain unpublished—until December 31, 2002
3. for works created before but published after January 1, 1978, date of copyright expiration may be extended to as late as 2027 so that the Copyright Office must be contacted for precise information on these works.

First Sale Doctrine— allows the resale or loan of a copy of a copyrighted work after it is first sold, without payment of an additional fee to the copyright holder. The doctrine allows libraries to lend books, videotapes, and software.

Fixation of a work—occurs when its embodiment in a copy or phonorecord, by or under the authority of the author, is sufficiently permanent or stable to permit it to be perceived, reproduced, or otherwise communicated for a period of more than transitory duration. A work consisting of sounds, images, or both, that are being transmitted, is fixed if a fixation of the work is being made simultaneously with its transmission.

Infringement—unauthorized, unexempted use of a work by one other than the copyright holder.

Instructional Text—a literary, pictorial, or graphic work prepared for publication and with the purpose of use in systematic instructional activities.

Joint work—one prepared by two or more authors with the intention that their contributions be merged into inseparable or interdependent parts of a unitary whole.

Literary works—works, other than audiovisual works, expressed in words, numbers, or other verbal or numerical symbols or indicia, regardless of the nature of the material objects (such as books, periodicals, manuscripts, phonorecords, film, tapes, disks, or cards) in which they are embodied.

Supplementary Work—prepared for publication as a secondary adjunct to a work by another author for the purpose of introducing, concluding, illustrating, explaining, revising, commenting on, or assisting in the use of the other work, such as forewords, afterwords, pictorials illustrations, maps, charts, tables, editorial notes, musical arrangements, answer material for tests, bibliographies, appendixes, and indexes.

Motion pictures—audiovisual works consisting of a series of related images which, when shown in succession, impart an impression of motion, together with accompanying sounds, if any.

Perform—to recite, render, play, dance, or act a work, either directly or by means of any device or process or, in the case of motion picture or other audiovisual works, to show its images in any sequence or to make the sound accompanying it audible.

Pictorial, graphic, and sculptural works—two- and three-dimensional works of fine, graphic, and applied art, photographs, prints and art reproductions, maps, globes, charts, diagrams, models, and technical drawings, including architectural plans. Such works include works of artistic craftsmanship insofar as their form but not their mechanical or utilitarian aspects are concerned. The design of a useful article shall be considered a pictorial, graphic, or sculptural work only if, and only to the extent that, such design incorporates pictorial, graphic, or sculptural features that can be identified separately from, and are capable of existing independently of, the utilitarian aspects of the article.

Publication—the distribution of copies or phonorecords of a work to the public by sale or other transfer of ownership, or by rental, lease, or lending. The offering to distribute copies or phonorecords to a group of persons for purposes of further distribution, public performance, or public display, constitutes publication. A public performance or display of a work does not of itself constitute publication. To perform or display a work "publicly" means

1. to perform or display it at a place open to the public or at any place where a substantial number of persons outside a normal circle of a family and its social acquaintances is gathered; or
2. to transmit or otherwise communicate a performance or display of the work to a place specified by clause 1 or to the public, by means of any device or process, whether the members of the public capable of receiving the performance or display receive it in the same place or in separate places and at the same or different times.

Sound recordings—works that result from the fixation of a series of musical, spoken, or other sounds, but not including the sounds accompanying a motion picture or other audiovisual work, regardless of the nature of the material objects, such as disks, tapes, or other phonorecords, in which they are embodied.

Transfer of copyright ownership—an assignment, mortgage, exclusive license, or any other conveyance, alienation, or hypothecation of a copyright or of any of the exclusive rights comprised in a copyright, whether or not it is limited in time or place of effect, but not including a nonexclusive license.

Transmit—to communicate a performance or display by any device or process whereby images or sounds are received beyond the place from which they are sent.

United States—in a geographical sense, comprising the 50 states, the District of Columbia, the Commonwealth of Puerto Rico, and the organized territories under the jurisdiction of the U.S. government.

United States as country of origin—the country of origin of a Berne Convention work is the United States if

1. for a published work, the work is first published
   a. in the United States;
   b. adhering to the Berne Convention, whose law grants a term of copyright protection that is the same or longer than the term provided in the United States;
   c. simultaneously in the United States and a foreign nation that does not adhere to the Berne Convention; or
   d. in a foreign nation that does not adhere to the Berne Convention, and all of the authors of the work are nationals, domiciliaries, or habitual residents of, or in the case of an audiovisual work legal entities with headquarters in, the United States;
2. in the case of an unpublished work, all the authors of the work are nationals, domiciliaries, or habitual residents of the United States,

or, in the case of an unpublished audiovisual work, all the authors are legal entities with headquarters in, the United States; or

3. in the case of pictorial, graphic, or sculptural work incorporated in a building or structure, the building or structure is located in the United States.

Useful article—an item having an intrinsic utilitarian function that is not merely to portray the appearance of the article or to convey information. An article that is a normal part of a useful article is considered a "useful article."

Widow, Widower—author's surviving spouse under the law of the author's domicile at the time of his or her death, whether or not the spouse has later remarried.

Work of visual art—

1. a painting, drawing, print, or sculpture, existing in a single copy, in a limited edition of 200 copies or fewer that are signed and consecutively numbered by the author, or, in the case of a sculpture, in multiple cast, carved, or fabricated sculptures of 200 or fewer that are consecutively numbered by the author and bear the signature or other identifying mark of the author; or
2. a still photographic image produced for exhibition purposes only, existing in a single copy that is signed by the author, or in a limited edition of 200 copies or fewer that are signed and consecutively numbered by the author.

A work of visual art does not include

1. any poster, map, globe, chart, technical drawing, diagram, model, applied art, motion picture or other audiovisual work, book, magazine, newspaper, periodical, database, electronic information service, electronic publication, or similar publication;
2. any work made for hire; or
3. any work not subject to copyright protection under Title 17.

Work of the U.S. government—a work prepared by an officer or employee of the U.S. government as part of that person's official duties. Such a work cannot be copyrighted.

Work for hire—

1. a work prepared by an employee within the scope of his or her employment; or
2. a work specially ordered or commissioned for use as a contribution to a collective work, as a part of a motion picture or other audiovisual work, as a translation, as a supplementary work, as a compilation, as an instructional text, as a test, as answer material for a test, or as an atlas, if the parties expressly agree in a written instrument signed by them that the work shall be considered a work made for hire.

Appendix A:
Library Copyright
Warning Notices

I. DISPLAY WARNING OF COPYRIGHT

[To Be Displayed at Place Where Interlibrary Loan Orders are Taken]

   37 CFR §201.14(b). A Display Warning of Copyright and an Order Warning of Copyright shall consist of a verbatim reproduction of the following notice, printed in such size and form and displayed in such manner as to comply with paragraph (c) of this section:

NOTICE WARNING CONCERNING COPYRIGHT RESTRICTIONS

The copyright law of the United States (Title 17, United States Code) governs the making of photocopies or other reproductions of copyrighted material.

Under certain conditions specified in the law, libraries and archives are authorized to furnish a photocopy or other reproduction. One of these specific conditions is that the photocopy or reproduction is not to be "used for any purpose other than private study, scholarship, or research." If a user makes a request for, or later uses, a photocopy or reproduction for purposes in excess of "fair use," that user may be liable for copyright infringement.

This institution reserves the right to refuse to accept a copying order if, in its judgment, fulfillment of the order would involve violation of copyright law.

37 CFR §201.14(c). Form and manner of use. (1) A Display Warning of Copyright shall be printed on heavy paper or other durable material in type at least 18 points in size, and shall be displayed prominently, in such manner and location as to be clearly visible, legible, and comprehensible to a casual observer within the immediate vicinity of the place where orders are accepted.

II. WARNING OF COPYRIGHT
[To Be Placed on or near Photocopier]

NOTICE:
THE COPYRIGHT LAW OF THE UNITED STATES (TITLE 17 U.S. CODE) GOVERNS THE MAKING OF PHOTOCOPIES OR OTHER REPRODUCTIONS OF COPYRIGHTED MATERIAL. THE PERSON USING THIS EQUIPMENT IS LIABLE FOR ANY INFRINGEMENT.

Note: there is no specific requirement except that

> ... such equipment display a notice that the making of a copy may be subject to the copyright law. 17 U.S.C. §108(f)(1).

It is recommended that type be at least 18 points in size.

III. WARNING OF COPYRIGHT FOR SOFTWARE LENDING BY NONPROFIT LIBRARIES

§201.24 Warning of copyright for software lending by nonprofit libraries.

(a) *Definition*. A Warning of Copyright for Software Rental is a notice under paragraph (b)(2)(A) of section 109 of the Copyright Act, title 17 of the United States Code, as amended by the Computer Software Rental Amendments Act of 1990, Public Law 101-650. As required by that paragraph, the "Warning of Copyright for Software Rental" shall be affixed to the package that contains the computer program which is lent by a nonprofit library for nonprofit purposes.

(b) *Contents.* A Warning of Copyright for Software Rental shall consist of a verbatim reproduction of the following notice, printed in such size and form and affixed in such manner as to comply with paragraph (c) of this section.

Notice: Warning of Copyright Restrictions
The copyright law of the United States (Title 17, United States Code) governs the reproduction, distribution, adaptation, public performance, and public display of copyrighted material.

Under certain circumstances specified in law, nonprofit libraries are authorized to lend, lease or rent copies of computer programs to patrons on a nonprofit basis and for nonprofit purposes. Any person who makes an unauthorized copy or adaptation of the computer program, or redistributes the loan copy, or publicly performs or displays the computer program, except as permitted by title 17 of the United States Code, may be liable for copyright infringement.

This institution reserves the right to refuse to fulfill a loan request if, in its judgment, fulfillment of the request would lead to violation of the copyright law.

(c) *Form and manner of use.* A Warning of Copyright for Software Rental shall be affixed to the package that contains the copy of the computer program, which is the subject of a library loan to patrons, by means of a label cemented, gummed, or otherwise durably attached to the copies or to a box, reel, cartridge, cassette, or other container used as a permanent receptacle for the copy of the computer program. The notice shall be printed in such manner as to be clearly legible, comprehensible, and readily apparent to a casual user of the computer program.

[56 FR 7812, Feb. 26, 1991]

IV. AN ORDER WARNING OF COPYRIGHT

37 C.F.R §201.14(a)(2). . . . the "Order Warning of Copyright" is to be included on printed forms supplied by certain libraries and archives and used by their patrons for ordering copies or phonorecords.

37 C.F.R §201.14(b)(2). An Order Warning of Copyright shall be printed within a box located prominently on the order form itself, either on the front side of the form or immediately adjacent to the space calling for the name or signature of the person using the form. The notice shall be printed in type size no smaller than that used predominantly throughout the form, and in no case shall the type size be smaller than 8 points. The notice shall be printed in such manner as to be clearly legible, comprehensible, and readable apparent to a casual reader of the form.

Appendix B: Exclusive Rights of Copyright Owners

SEC. 106. EXCLUSIVE RIGHTS IN COPYRIGHTED WORKS

Subject to sections 107 through 120, the owner of copyright under this title has the exclusive rights to do and to authorize any of the following:

(1) to reproduce the copyrighted work in copies or phonorecords;

(2) to prepare derivative works based upon the copyrighted work;

(3) to distribute copies or phonorecords of the copyrighted work to the public by sale or other transfer of ownership, or by rental, lease, or lending;

(4) in the case of literary, musical, dramatic, and choreographic works, pantomimes, and motion pictures and other audiovisual works, to perform the copyrighted work publicly; and

(5) in the case of literary, musical, dramatic, and choreographic works, pantomimes, and pictorial, graphic, or sculptural works, including the individual images of a motion picture or other audiovisual work, to display the copyrighted work publicly.

[Public Law 104–39 §2 (November 1, 1995) added:]

(6) in the case of sound recordings, to perform the copyrighted work publicly by means of a digital audio transmission.

Appendix C:
Limitations on the Rights of Copyright Owners
(OF PARTICULAR INTEREST TO EDUCATORS, LIBRARIANS, AND RESEARCHERS)

SECTION 108 OF THE COPYRIGHT LAW

(a) Notwithstanding the provisions of section 106, it is not an infringement of copyright for a library or archive, or any of its employees acting within the scope of their employment, to reproduce no more than one copy or phonorecord of a work, or to distribute such copy or phonorecord, under the conditions specified by this section, if—

    (1) the reproduction or distribution is made without any purpose of direct or indirect commercial advantage;

    (2) the collections of the library or archives are (i) open to the public, or (ii) available not only to researchers affiliated with the library or archives or with the institution of which it is a part, but also to other persons doing research in a specialized field; and

    (3) the reproduction or distribution of the work includes a notice of copyright.

(b) The rights of reproduction and distribution under this section apply to a copy or phonorecord of an unpublished work duplicated in facsimile form solely for purposes of preservation and security or for deposit for research use in another library or archives of the type described by clause (2) of subsection (a), if the copy or phonorecord reproduced is currently in the collections of the library or archives.

(c) The rights of reproduction under this section apply to a copy or phonorecord of a published work duplicated in facsimile form solely for the purpose of replacement of a copy or phonorecord that is damaged, deteriorating, lost, or stolen, if the library or archives has, after a reasonable effort, determined that an unused replacement cannot be obtained at a fair price.

(d) The rights of reproduction and distribution under this section apply to a copy, made from the collection of a library or archive where the user makes his or her request or from that of another library or archives, of no more than one article or other contribution to a copyrighted collection or periodical issue, or to a copy or phonorecord of a small part of any other copyrighted work, if:

   (1) the copy or phonorecord becomes the property of the user, and the library or archives has had no notice that the copy or phonorecord would be used for any purpose other than private study, scholarship, or research; and

   (2) the library or archives displays prominently, at the place where orders are accepted, and includes on its order form, a warning of copyright in accordance with requirements that the Register of Copyrights shall prescribe by regulation.

(e) The rights of reproduction and distribution under this section apply to the entire work, or to a substantial part of it, made from the collection of a library or archives where the user makes his or her request or from that of another library or archives, if the library or archives has first determined, on the basis of a reasonable investigation, that a copy or phonorecord of the copyrighted work cannot be obtained at a fair price, if—

   (1) the copy or phonorecord becomes the property of the user, and the library or archives has had no notice that the copy or phonorecord would be used for any purpose other than private study, scholarship, or research; and

   (2) the library or archives displays prominently, at the place where orders are accepted, and includes on its order form, a warning of copyright in accordance with requirements that the Register of Copyright shall prescribe by regulation.

(f) Nothing in this section

   (1) shall be construed to impose liability for copyright infringement upon a library or archives or its employees for the unsupervised use of reproducing equipment lo-

cated on its premises: Provided, That such equipment displays a notice that the making of a copy may be subject to the copyright law;

(2) excuses a person who uses such reproducing equipment or who requests a copy or phonorecord under subsection (d) from liability for copyright infringement for any such act, or for any later use of such copy or phonorecord, if it exceeds fair use as provided by section 107.

(3) of subsection (a); or

(4) in any way affects the rights of fair use as provided by section 107, or any contractual obligations assumed at any time by the library or archives when it obtained a copy or phonorecord of a work in its collections.

(g) The rights of reproduction and distribution under this section extend to the isolated and unrelated reproduction or distribution of a single copy or phonorecord of the same material on separate occasions, but do not extend to cases where the library or archives, or its employee—

(1) is aware or has substantial reason to believe that it is engaging in the related or concerted reproduction or distribution of multiple copies or phonorecords of the same material, whether made on one occasion or over a period of time, and whether intended for aggregate use by one or more individuals or for separate use by the individual members of a group; or

(2) engages in the systematic reproduction or distribution of single or multiple copies or phonorecords of material described in subsection (d): Provided, That nothing in this clause prevents a library or archives from participating in interlibrary arrangements that do not have, as their purpose or effect, that the library or archives receiving such copies or phonorecords for distribution does so in such aggregate quantities as to substitute for a subscription to or purchase of such work.

(h) The rights of reproduction and distribution under this section do not apply to a musical work, a pictorial, graphic or sculptural work, or a motion picture or other audiovisual work other than an audiovisual work dealing with news, except that no such limitation shall apply with respect to rights granted by subsections (b) and (c), or with respect to pictorial or graphic works published as illustrations, diagrams, or similar adjuncts to works of which copies are reproduced or distributed in accordance with subsections (d) and (e).

(i) **[REPEALED]** Five years from the effective date of this Act, and at five-year intervals thereafter, the Register of Copyrights, after consulting with representatives of authors, book and periodical publishers, and other owners of copyrighted materials, and with representatives of library users and librarians, shall submit to the Congress a report setting forth the extent to which this section has achieved the intended statutory balancing of the rights of creators, and the needs of users. The report should also describe any problems that may have arisen, and present legislative or other recommendations, if warranted.

SEC. 109. LIMITATIONS ON EXCLUSIVE RIGHTS: EFFECT OF TRANSFER OF PARTICULAR COPY OR PHONORECORD

(a) Notwithstanding the provisions of section 106(3), the owner of a particular copy or phonorecord lawfully made under this title, or any person authorized by such owner, is entitled, without the authority of the copyright owner, to sell or otherwise dispose of the possession of that copy or phonorecord.

(b)(1)(A) Notwithstanding the provisions of subsection (a), unless authorized by the owners of copyright in the sound recording or the owner of copyright in a computer program (including any tape, disk, or other medium embodying such program), and in the case of a sound recording in the musical works embodied therein, neither the owner of a particular phonorecord nor any person in possession of a particular copy of a computer program (including any tape, disk, or other medium embodying such program), may, for the purposes of direct or indirect commercial advantage, dispose of, or authorize the disposal of, the possession of that phonorecord or computer program (including any tape, disk, or other medium embodying such program) by rental, lease, or lending, or by any other act or practice in the nature of rental, lease, or lending. Nothing in the preceding sentence shall apply to the rental, lease, or lending of a phonorecord for nonprofit purposes by a nonprofit library or nonprofit educational institution. The transfer of possession of a lawfully made copy of a computer program by a nonprofit educational institution to another nonprofit educational institution or to faculty, staff, and students does not constitute rental, lease, or lending for direct or indirect commercial purposes under this subsection.

(B) This subsection does not apply to—

    (i) a computer program which is embodied in a machine or product and which cannot be copied during the ordinary operation or use of the machine or product; or

    (ii) a computer program embodied in or used in conjunction with a limited purpose computer that is designed for playing video games and may be designed for other purposes.

(C) Nothing in this subsection affects any provision of chapter 9 of this title.

(2) (A) Nothing in this subsection shall apply to the lending of a computer program for nonprofit purposes by a nonprofit library, if each copy of a computer program which is lent by such library has affixed to the packaging containing the program a warning of copyright in accordance with requirements that the Register of Copyrights shall prescribe by regulation.

(B) Not later than three years after the date of the enactment of the Computer Software Rental Amendments Act of 1990, and at such times thereafter as the Register of Copyright considers appropriate, the Register of Copyrights, after consultation with representatives of copyright owners and librarians, shall submit to the Congress a report stating whether this paragraph has achieved its intended purpose of maintaining the integrity of the copyright system while providing nonprofit libraries the capability to fulfill their function. Such report shall advise the Congress as to any information or recommendations that the Register of Copyrights considers necessary to carry out the purposes of this subsection.

(3) Nothing in this subsection shall affect any provision of the antitrust laws. For purposes of the preceding sentence, "antitrust laws" has the meaning given that term in the first section of the Clayton Act and includes section 5 of the Federal Trade Commission Act to the ex-

tent that section relates to unfair methods of competition.

(4) Any person who distributes a phonorecord or a copy of a computer program (including any tape, disk, or other medium embodying such program) in violation of paragraph (1) is an infringer of copyright under section 501 of this title and is subject to the remedies set forth in sections 502, 503, 504, 505, and 509. Such violation shall not be a criminal offense under section 506 or cause such person to be subject to the criminal penalties set forth in section 2319 of title 18.

(c) Notwithstanding the provisions of section 106(5), the owner of a particular copy lawfully made under this title, or any person authorized by such owner, is entitled, without the authority of the copyright owner, to display that copy publicly, either directly or by the projection of no more than one image at a time, to viewers present at the place where the copy is located.

(d) The privileges prescribed by subsections (a) and (c) do not, unless authorized by the copyright owner, extend to any person who has acquired possession of the copy or phonorecord from the copyright owner, by rental, lease, loan, or otherwise, without acquiring ownership of it.

(e) Notwithstanding the provisions of sections 106(4) and 106(5), in the case of an electronic audiovisual game intended for use in coin-operated equipment, the owner of a particular copy of such a game lawfully made under this title, is entitled, without the authority of the copyright owner of the game, to publicly perform or display that game in coin-operated equipment, except that this subsection shall not apply to any work of authorship embodied in the audiovisual game if the copyright owner of the electronic audiovisual game is not also the copyright owner of the work of authorship.

[Section 109 has been since amended by P.L. 103–465.]

SEC. 110. LIMITATIONS ON EXCLUSIVE RIGHTS: EXEMPTION OF CERTAIN PERFORMANCES AND DISPLAYS

Notwithstanding the provisions of section 106, the following are not infringements of copyright:

(1) performance or display of a work by instructors or pupils in the course of face-to-face teaching activities of a nonprofit educational institution, in a classroom or similar place devoted to instruction, unless, in the case of a motion picture or other audiovisual work, the performance, or the display of individual images, is given by means of a copy that was not lawfully made under this title, and that the person responsible for the performance knew or had reason to believe was not lawfully made;

(2) performance of a nondramatic literary or musical work or display of a work, by or in the course of a transmission, if—

(A) the performance or display is a regular part of the systematic instructional activities of a governmental body or a nonprofit educational institution; and

(B) the performance or display is directly related and of material assistance to the teaching content of the transmission; and

(C) the transmission is made primarily for—

(i)   reception in classrooms or similar places normally devoted to instruction, or

(ii) reception by persons to whom the transmission is directed because their disabilities or other special circumstances prevent their attendance in classrooms or similar places normally devoted to instruction, or

(iii) reception by officers or employees of governmental bodies as a part of their official duties or employment;

(3) performance of a nondramatic literary or musical work or of a dramatico-musical work of a religious nature, or display of a work, in the course of services at a place of worship or other religious assembly;

(4) performance of a nondramatic literary or musical work otherwise than in a transmission to the public, without any purpose of direct or indirect commercial advantage and without payment of any fee or other compensation for the performance to any of its performers, promoters, or organizers, if—

    (A) there is no direct or indirect admission charge; or

    (B) the proceeds, after deducting the reasonable costs of producing the performance, are used exclusively for educational, religious, or charitable purposes and not for private financial gain, except where the copyright owner has served notice of objection to the performance under the following conditions:

        (i) the notice shall be in writing and signed by the copyright owner or such owner's duly authorized agent; and

        (ii) the notice shall be served on the person responsible for the performance at least seven days before the date of the performance, and shall state the reasons for the objection; and

        (iii) the notice shall comply, in form, content, and manner of service, with requirements that the Register of Copyrights shall prescribe by regulation;

(5) communication of a transmission embodying a performance or display of a work by the public reception of the transmission on a single receiving apparatus of a kind commonly used in private homes, unless—

    (A) a direct charge is made to see or hear the transmission; or

    (B) the transmission thus received is further transmitted to the public;

(6) performance of a nondramatic musical work by a governmental body or a nonprofit agricultural or horticultural organization, in the course of an annual agricultural or horticultural fair or exhibition conducted by such body or organization; the exemption provided by this clause shall extend to any liability for copyright infringement that would otherwise be imposed on such

body or organization, under doctrines of vicarious liability or related infringement, for a performance by a concessionnaire, business establishment, or other person at such fair or exhibition, but shall not excuse any such person from liability for the performance;

(7) performance of a nondramatic musical work by a vending establishment open to the public at large without any direct or indirect admission charge, where the sole purpose of the performance is to promote the retail sale of copies or phonorecords of the work, and the performance is not transmitted beyond the place where the establishment is located and is within the immediate area where the sale is occurring;

(8) performance of a nondramatic literary work, by or in the course of a transmission specifically designed for and primarily directed to blind or other handicapped persons who are unable to read normal printed material as a result of their handicap, or deaf or other handicapped persons who are unable to hear the aural signals accompanying a transmission of visual signals, if the performance is made without any purpose of direct or indirect commercial advantage and its transmission is made through the facilities of: (i) a governmental body; or (ii) a noncommercial educational broadcast station (as defined in section 397 of title 47); or (iii) a radio subcarrier authorization (as defined in 47 CFR 73.293–73.295 and 73.593–73.595); or (iv) a cable system (as defined in section 111(f)).

(9) performance on a single occasion of a dramatic literary work published at least ten years before the date of the performance, by or in the course of a transmission specifically designed for and primarily directed to blind or other handicapped persons who are unable to read normal printed material as a result of their handicap, if the performance is made without any purpose of direct or indirect commercial advantage and its transmission is made through the facilities of a radio subcarrier authorization referred to in clause (8)(iii), Provided, That the provisions of this clause shall not be applicable to more than one performance of the same work by the same performers or under the auspices of the same organization.

(10) notwithstanding paragraph 4 above, the following is not an infringement of copyright: performance of a nondramatic literary or musical work in the course of a social function which is organized and promoted by a nonprofit veterans' organization or a nonprofit fraternal organization to which the general public is not invited, but not including the invitees of the organizations, if the proceeds from the performance, after deducting the reasonable costs of producing the performance, are used exclusively for charitable purposes and not for financial gain. For purposes of this section the social functions of any college or university fraternity or sorority shall not be included unless the social function is held solely to raise funds for a specific charitable purpose.

SEC. 117. LIMITATIONS ON EXCLUSIVE RIGHTS: COMPUTER PROGRAMS

Notwithstanding the provisions of section 106, it is not an infringement for the owner of a copy of a computer program to make or authorize the making of another copy or adaptation of that computer program provided:

(1) that such new copy or adaptation is created as an essential step in the utilization of the computer program in conjunction with a machine and that it is used in no other manner, or

(2) that such new copy or adaptation is for archival purposes only and that all archival copies are destroyed in the event that continued possession of the computer program should cease to be rightful.

Any exact copies prepared in accordance with the provisions of this section may be leased, sold, or otherwise transferred, along with the copy from which such copies were prepared, only as part of the lease, sale, or other transfer of all rights in the program. Adaptations so prepared may be transferred only with the authorization of the copyright owner.

Appendix D: Legislative Materials on Section 108

I. EXCERPTS FROM SENATE REPORT ON SECTION 108

The following excerpts are reprinted from the 1975 Senate Report on the new copyright law (Senate Report No. 94–473, pages 67–71). Where the discussions of particular points are generally similar in the two Reports, the passages from the later House Report are reprinted. Where the discussion of particular points is substantially different, passages from both reports are reprinted.

a. Senate Report: Discussion of Libraries and Archives in Profit-Making Institutions

The limitation of section 108 to reproduction and distribution by libraries and archives "without any purpose of direct or indirect commercial advantage" is intended to preclude a library or archives in a profit-making organization from providing photocopies of copyrighted materials to employees engaged in furtherance of the organization's commercial enterprise, unless such copying qualifies as a fair use, or the organization has obtained the necessary copyright licenses. A commercial organization should purchase the number of copies of a work that it requires, or obtain the consent of the copyright owner to the making of the photocopies.

b. Senate Report: Discussion of Multiple Copies and Systematic Reproduction

Multiple copies and systematic reproduction

Subsection (g) provides that the rights granted by this section extend only to the "isolated and unrelated reproduction of a single copy," but this section does not authorize the related or concerted reproduction of multiple copies of the same material whether made on one occasion or over a period of time, and whether intended for aggregate use by one individual or for separate use by the individual members of a group. For example, if a college professor instructs his class to read an article from a copyrighted journal, the school library would not be permitted, under subsection (g), to reproduce copies of the article for the members of the class.

Subsection (g) also provides that section 108 does not authorize the systematic reproduction or distribution of copies or phonorecords of articles or other contributions to copyrighted collections or periodicals or of small parts of other copyrighted works whether or not multiple copies are reproduced or distributed. Systematic reproduction or distribution occurs when a library makes copies of such materials available to other libraries or to groups of users under formal or informal arrangements whose purpose or effect is to have the reproducing library serve as their source of such material. Such systematic reproduction and distribution, as distinguished from isolated and unrelated reproduction or distribution, may substitute the copies reproduced by the source library for subscriptions or reprints or other copies which the receiving libraries or users might otherwise have purchased for themselves, from the publisher or the licensed reproducing agencies.

While it is not possible to formulate specific definitions of "systematic copying," the following examples serve to illustrate some of the copying prohibited by subsection (g).

(1) A library with a collection of journals in biology informs other libraries with similar collections that it will maintain and build its own collection and will make copies of articles from these journals available to them and their patrons on request. Accordingly, the other libraries discontinue or refrain from purchasing subscriptions to these journals and fulfill their patrons' requests for articles by obtaining photocopies from the source library.

(2) A research center employing a number of scientists and technicians subscribes to one or two copies of needed periodicals. By reproducing photocopies of articles the center is able to make the material in these periodicals available to its staff in the same manner which otherwise would have required multiple subscriptions.

(3) Several branches of a library system agree that one branch will subscribe to particular journals in lieu of each branch purchasing its own subscriptions, and the one subscribing branch will reproduce copies of articles from the publication for users of the other branches.

The committee believes that section 108 provides an appropriate statutory balancing of the rights of creators, and the needs of users. However, neither a statute nor legislative history can specify precisely which library photocopying practices constitute the making of "single copies" as distinguished from "systematic reproduction." Isolated single spontaneous requests must be distinguished from "systematic reproduction." The photocopying needs of such operations as multi-county regional systems must be met. The committee therefore recommends that representatives of authors, book and periodical publishers and other owners of copyrighted material meet with the library community to formulate photocopying guidelines to assist library patrons and employees. Concerning library photocopying practices not authorized by this legislation, the committee recommends that workable clearance and licensing procedures be developed.

It is still uncertain how far a library may go under the Copyright Act of 1909 in supplying a photocopy of copyrighted material in its collection. The recent case of *The Williams and Wilkins Company v The United States* failed to significantly illuminate the application of the fair use doctrine to library photocopying practices. Indeed, the opinion of the Court of Claims said the Court was engaged in "a 'holding operation' in the interim period before Congress enacted its preferred solution."

While the several opinions in the *Wilkins* case have given the Congress little guidance as to the current state of the law on fair use, these opinions provide additional support for the balanced resolution of the photocopying issue adopted by the Senate last year in S. 1361 and preserved in section 108 of this legislation. As the Court of Claims opinion succinctly stated "there is much to be said on all sides." In adopting these provisions on library photocopying, the committee is aware that through such programs as those of the National Commission on Libraries and Information Science there will be a significant evolution in the functioning and services of libraries. To consider the possible need for changes in copyright law and procedures as a result of new technology, a National Commission on New Technological Uses of Copyrighted Words has been established (Public Law 93–573).

II. EXCERPTS FROM HOUSE REPORT ON SECTION 108

The following excerpts are reprinted from the House Report on the new copyright law (House Report No. 94–1476, pages 74–79). All of the House Report's discussion of section 108 is reprinted here; similarities and differences between the House and Senate Reports on particular points will be noted below.

a. House Report: Introductory Statement

[This paragraph is substantially the same in the Senate and House Reports.]
Notwithstanding the exclusive rights of the owners of copyright, section 108 provides that under certain conditions it is not an infringement of copyright for a library or archives, or any of its employees acting within the scope of their employment, to reproduce or distribute not more than one copy or phonorecord of a work, provided (1) the reproduction or distribution is made without any purpose of direct or indirect commercial advantage and (2) the collections of the library or archives are open to the public or available not only to researchers affiliated with the library or archives, but also to other persons doing research in a specialized field, and (3) the reproduction of distribution of the work includes a notice of copyright.

b. House Report: Discussion of Libraries and Archives in Profit-Making Institutions

[The Senate and House Reports differ substantially on this point. The Senate Report's discussion is reprinted above.]

Under this provision, a purely commercial enterprise could not establish a collection of copyrighted works, call itself a library or archive, and engage in for-profit reproduction and distribution of photocopies. Similarly, it would not be possible for a non-profit institution, by means of contractual arrangements with a commercial copying enterprise, to authorize the enterprise to carry out copying and distribution functions that would be exempt if conducted by the non-profit institution itself.

The reference to "indirect commercial advantage" has raised questions as to the status of photocopying done by or for libraries or archival collections within industrial, profitmaking, or proprietary institutions (such as the research and development departments of chemical, pharmaceutical, automobile, and oil corporations, the library of a proprietary hospital, the collections owned by a law or medical partnership, etc.).

There is a direct interrelationship between this problem and the prohibitions against "multiple" and "systematic" photocopying in section 108 (g) (1) and (2). Under section 108, a library in a profit-making organization would not be authorized to:

(a) use a single subscription or copy to supply its employees with multiple copies of material relevant to their work; or
(b) use a single subscription or copy to supply its employees, on request, with single copies of material relevant to their work, where the arrangement is "systematic" in the sense of deliberately substituting photocopying for subscription or purchase; or
(c) use "interlibrary loan" arrangements for obtaining photocopies in such aggregate quantities as to substitute for subscriptions or purchase of material needed by employees in their work.

Moreover, a library in a profit-making organization could not evade these obligations by installing reproducing equipment on its premises for unsupervised use by the organization's staff.

Isolated, spontaneous making of single photocopies by a library in a for-profit organization, without any systematic effort to substitute photocopying for subscriptions or purchases, would be covered by section 108, even though the copies are furnished to the employees of the organization for use in their work. Similarly, for-profit libraries could participate in interlibrary arrangements for exchange of photocopies, as long as the reproduction or distribution was not "systematic." These activities, by themselves, would ordinarily not be considered "for direct or indirect commercial advantage," since the "advantage" referred to in this clause must attach to the immediate commercial motivation behind the reproduction or distribution itself, rather than to the ultimate profit-making motivation behind the enterprise in which the library is located. On the other hand, section 108 would not excuse reproduction or distribution if there were a commercial motive behind the actual making or distributing of the copies, if multiple copies were made or distributed, or if the photocopying activities were "systematic" in the sense that their aim was to substitute for subscriptions or purchases.

c. House Report: Rights of Reproduction and Distribution Under Section 108

[*The following paragraphs are closely similar in the Senate and House Reports.*]
The rights of reproduction and distribution under section 108 apply in the following circumstances:

Archival reproduction
Subsection (b) authorizes the reproduction and distribution of a copy or phonorecord of an unpublished work duplicated in facsimile form solely for purposes of preservation and security, or for deposit for research use in another library or archives, if the copy or phonorecord reproduced is currently in the collections of the first library or archives. Only unpublished works could be reproduced under this exemption, but the right would extend to any type of work, including photographs, motion pictures and sound recordings. Under this exemption, for example, a repository could make photocopies of manuscripts by microfilm or electrostatic process, but could not reproduce the work in "machine-readable" language for storage in an information system.

Replacement of damaged copy
Subsection (c) authorizes the reproduction of a published work duplicated in facsimile form solely for the purpose of replacement of a copy or phonorecord that is damaged, deteriorating, lost or stolen, if the library or archives has, after a reasonable effort, determined that an unused replacement cannot be obtained at a fair price. The scope and nature of a reasonable investigation to determine that an unused replacement cannot be obtained will vary according to the circumstances of a particular situation. It will always require recourse to commonly-known trade sources in the United States, and in the normal situation also to the publisher or

other copyright owner (if such owner can be located at the address listed in the copyright registration), or an authorized reproducing service.

Articles and small excerpts
Subsection (d) authorizes the reproduction and distribution of a copy of not more than one article or other contribution to a copyrighted collection or periodical issue, or of a copy or phonorecord of a small part of any other copyrighted work. The copy or phonorecord may be made by the library where the user makes his request or by another library pursuant to an interlibrary loan. It is further required that the copy become the property of the user, that the library or archives have no notice that the copy would be used for any purposes other than private study, scholarship or research, and that the library or archives display prominently at the place where reproduction requests are accepted, and includes in its order form, a warning of copyright in accordance with requirements that the Register of Copyrights shall prescribe by regulation.

Out-of-print works
Subsection (e) authorizes the reproduction and distribution of a copy or phonorecord of an entire work under certain circumstances, if it has been established that a copy cannot be obtained at a fair price. The copy may be made by the library where the user makes his request or by another library pursuant to an interlibrary loan. The scope and nature of a reasonable investigation to determine that an unused copy cannot be obtained will vary according to the circumstances of a particular situation. It will always require recourse to commonly-known trade sources in the United States, and in the normal situation also to the publisher or other copyright owner (if the owner can be located at the address listed in the copyright registration), or an authorized reproducing service. It is further required that the copy become the property of the user, that the library or archives have no notice that the copy would be used for any purpose other than private study, scholarship, or research, and that the library or archives display prominently at the place where reproduction requests are accepted, and include on its order form, a warning of copyright in accordance with requirements that the Register of Copyrights shall prescribe by regulation.

d. House Report: General Exemptions for Libraries and Archives

[Parts of the following paragraphs are substantially similar in the Senate and House Reports. Differences in the House Report on certain points reflect certain amendments in section 108(f) and elsewhere in the Copyright Act.]

General exemptions

Clause (1) of subsection (f) specifically exempts a library or archives or its employees from liability for the unsupervised use of reproducing equipment located on its premises, provided that the reproducing equipment displays a notice that the making of a copy may be subject to the copyright law. Clause (2) of subsection (f) makes clear that this exemption of the library or archives does not extend to the person using such equipment or requesting such copy if the use exceeds fair use. Insofar as such person is concerned the copy or phonorecord made is not considered "lawfully" made for purposes of sections 109, 110 or other provisions of the title.

Clause (3) provides that nothing in section 108 is intended to limit the reproduction and distribution by lending of a limited number of copies and excerpts of an audiovisual news program. This exemption is intended to apply to the daily newscasts of the national television networks, which report the major events of the day. It does not apply to documentary (except documentary programs involving news reporting as that term is used in section 107), magazine-format or other public affairs broadcasts dealing with subjects of general interest to the viewing public. The clause was first added to the revision bill in 1974 by the adoption of an amendment proposed by Senator Baker. It is intended to permit libraries and archives, subject to the general conditions of this section, to make off-the-air videotape recordings of daily network newscasts for limited distribution to scholars and researchers for use in research purposes. As such, it is an adjunct to the American Television and Radio Archive established in Section 113 of the Act which will be the principal repository for television broadcast material, including news broadcasts. The inclusion of language indicating that such material may only be distributed by lending by the library or archive is intended to preclude performance, copying, or sale, whether or not for profit, by the recipient of a copy of a television broadcast taped off-the-air pursuant to this clause.

Clause (4), in addition to asserting that nothing contained in section 108 "affects the right of fair use as provided by section 107," also provides that the right of reproduction granted by this section does not override any contractual arrangements assumed by a library or archives when it obtains a work for its collections. For example, if there is an express contractual prohibition against reproduction for any purpose, this legislation shall not be construed as justifying a violation of the contract. This clause is intended to encompass the situation where an individual makes papers, manuscripts or other works available to a library with the understanding that they will not be reproduced.

It is the intent of this legislation that a subsequent unlawful use by a user of a copy or phonorecord of a work lawfully made by a library, shall not make the library liable for such improper use.

e. House Report: Discussion of Multiple Copies and Systematic Reproduction

[The Senate and House Reports differ substantially on this point. The Senate Report's discussion is reprinted above.]

Multiple copies and systematic reproduction
Subsection (g) provides that the rights granted by this section extend only to the "isolated and unrelated reproduction of a single copy or phonorecord of the same material on separate occasions." However, this section does not authorize the related or concerted reproduction of multiple copies or phonorecords of the same material, whether made on one occasion or over a period of time, and whether intended for aggregate use by one individual or for separate use by the individual members of a group.

With respect to material described in subsection (d)—articles or other contributions to periodicals or collections, and small parts of other copyrighted works—subsection (g)(2) provides that the exemptions of section 108 do not apply if the library or archive engages in "systematic reproduction or distribution of single or multiple copies or phonorecords." This provision in S.22 provoked a storm of controversy, centering around the extent to which the restrictions on "systematic" activities would prevent the continuation and development of interlibrary networks and other arrangements involving the exchange of photocopies. After thorough consideration, the Committee amended section 108 (g)(2) to add the following proviso:

Provided, that nothing in this clause prevents a library or archives from participating in interlibrary arrangements that do not have, as their purpose or effect, that the library or archives receiving such copies or phonorecords for distribution does so in such aggregate quantities as to substitute for a subscription to or purchase of such work.

In addition, the Committee added a new subsection (i) to section 108, requiring the Register of Copyrights, five years from the effective date of the new Act and at five-year intervals thereafter, to report to Congress upon "the extent to which this section has achieved the intended statutory balancing of the rights of creators, and the needs of users," and to make appropriate legislative or other recommendations. As noted in connection with section 107, the Committee also amended section 504(c) in a way that would insulate librarians from unwarranted liability for copyright infringement; this amendment is discussed below.

The key phrases in the Committee's amendment of section 108(g)(2) are "aggregate quantities" and "substitute for a subscription to or purchase of" a work. To be implemented effectively in practice, these provisions will require the development and implementation of more-or-less specific guidelines establishing criteria to govern various situation.

The National Commission on New Technological Uses of Copyrighted Works (CONTU) offered to provide good offices in helping to develop these guidelines. This offer was accepted and, although the final text of guidelines has not yet been achieved, the Committee has reason to hope that, within the next month, some agreement can be reached on an initial set of guidelines covering practices under section 108(g)(2).

f. House Report: Discussion of Works Excluded

[The House Report's discussion of Section 108(h) is longer than the corresponding paragraph in the Senate Report, and reflects certain amendments in the subsection.]

Works excluded
Subsection (h) provides that the rights of reproduction and distribution under this section do not apply to a musical work, a pictorial, graphic or sculptural work, or a motion picture or other audiovisual work other than "an audiovisual work dealing with news." The latter term is intended as the equivalent in meaning of the phrase "audiovisual news program" in section 108(f)(3). The exclusions under subsection (h) do not apply to archival reproduction

under subsection (b), to replacement of damaged or lost copies or phonorecords under subsection (c), or to "pictorial or graphic works published as illustrations, diagrams, or similar adjuncts to works of which copies are reproduced or distributed in accordance with subsections (d) and (e)."

Although subsection (h) generally removes musical, graphic, and audiovisual works from the specific exemptions of section 108, it is important to recognize that the doctrine of fair use under section 107 remains fully applicable to the photocopying or other reproduction of such works. In the case of music, for example, it would be fair use for a scholar doing musicological research to have a library supply a copy of a portion of a score or to reproduce portions of a phonorecord of a work. Nothing in section 108 impairs the applicability of the fair use doctrine to a wide variety of situations involving photocopying or other reproduction by a library of copyrighted material in its collections, where the user requests the reproduction for legitimate scholarly or research purposes.

III. EXCERPTS FROM CONFERENCE REPORT

[The following excerpt is reprinted from the Report of the Conference Committee on the New Copyright Law (House Report No. 94–1733, pages 70–74).]

a. Conference Report: Introductory Discussion of Section 108

REPRODUCTION BY LIBRARIES AND ARCHIVES

Senate bill
Section 108 of the Senate bill dealt with a variety of situations involving photocopying and other forms of reproduction by libraries and archives. It specified the conditions under which single copies of copyrighted material can be noncommercially reproduced and distributed, but made clear that the privileges of a library or archive under the section do not apply where the reproduction or distribution is of multiple copies or is "systematic." Under subsection (f), the section was not to be construed as limited to the reproduction and distribution, by a library or archive meeting the basic criteria of the section, of a limited number of copies and excerpts of an audiovisual news program.

House bill
The House bill amended section 108 to make clear that, in cases involving interlibrary arrangements for the exchange of photocopies, the activity would not be considered "systematic" as long as the library or archive receiving the reproductions for distribution does not do so in such aggregate quantities as to substitute for a subscription to or purchase of the work. A new subsection (i) directed the Register of Copyrights, by the end of 1982 and at five-year intervals thereafter, to report on the practical success of the section in balancing the various interests, and to make recommendations for any needed changes. With respect to audiovisual news programs, the House bill limited the scope of the distribution privilege confirmed by section 108 (f)(3) to cases where the distribution takes the form of a loan.

b. Conference Report: Conference Committee Discussion of CONTU Guidelines on Photocopying and Interlibrary Arrangements

Conference substitute
The conference substitute adopts the provisions of section 108 as amended by the House bill. In doing so, the conferees have noted two letters dated September 22, 1976, sent respectively to John L. McClellan, Chairman of the Senate Judiciary Subcommittee on Patents, Trademarks, and Copyrights, and to Robert W. Kastenmeier, Chairman of the House Judiciary Subcommittee on Courts, Civil Liberties, and the Administration of Justice. The letters, from the Chairman of the national Commission on New Technological Uses of Copyrighted Works (CONTU), Stanley H. Fuld, transmitted a document consisting of "guidelines interpreting the provision in subsection 108(g)(2) of S.22, as approved by the House Committee on the Judiciary." Chairman Fuld's letters explain that, following lengthy consultations with the parties concerned, the Commission adopted these guidelines as fair and workable and with the hope that the conferees on S.22 may find that they merit inclusion in the conference report. The letters add that, although time did not permit securing signatures of the representatives of the principal library organizations or of the organizations representing publishers and authors on these guidelines, the Commission had received oral assurances from these representatives that the guidelines are acceptable to their organizations.

The conference committee understands that the guidelines are not intended as, and cannot be considered, explicit rules or directions governing any and all cases, now or in the future. It is recognized that their purpose is to provide guidance in the most commonly-encountered interlibrary photocopying situations, that they are not intended to be limiting or determinative in themselves or with respect to other situations, and that they deal with an evolving situation that will undoubtedly require their continuous reevaluation and adjustment. With these qualifications, the conference committee agrees that the guidelines are a reasonable interpretation of the proviso of section 108 (g)(2) in the most common situations to which they apply today.

c. Conference Report: Reprint of CONTU Guidelines on Photocopying and Interlibrary Arrangements

PHOTOCOPYING—INTERLIBRARY ARRANGEMENTS

Introduction
Subsection 108(g) (2) of the bill deals, among other things, with limits on interlibrary arrangements for photocopying. It prohibits systematic photocopying of copyrighted materials but permits interlibrary arrangements "that do not have, as their purposes or effect, that the library or archives receiving such copies or phonorecords for distribution does so in such aggregate quantities as to substitute for a subscription to or purchase of such work."

The National Commission on New Technological Uses of Copyrighted Works offered its good offices to the House and Senate subcommittees in bringing the interested parties together to see if agreement could be reached on what a realistic definition would be of "such aggregate quantities." The Commission consulted with the parties and suggested the interpretation which follows, on which there has been substantial agreement by the principal library, publisher, and author organizations. The Commission considers the guidelines which follow to be a workable and fair interpretation of the intent of the proviso portion of subsection 108 (g)(2).

These guidelines are intended to provide guidance in the application of section 108 to the most frequently encountered interlibrary case; a library's obtaining from another library, in lieu of interlibrary loan, copies of articles from relatively recent issues of periodicals—those published within five years prior to the date of the request. The guidelines do not specify what aggregate quantity of copies of an article or articles published in a periodical, the issue date of which is more than five years prior to the date when the request for the copy thereof is made, constitutes a substitute for a subscription to such periodical. The meaning of the proviso to subsection 108 (g)(2) in such case is left to future interpretation.

The point has been made that the present practice on interlibrary loans and use of photocopies in lieu of loans may be supplemented or even largely replaced by a system in which one or more agencies or institutions, public or private, exist for the specific purpose of providing a central source for photocopies. Of course, these guidelines would not apply to such a situation.

Guidelines for the Proviso of Subsection 108(g)(2)

1. As used in the proviso of subsection 108(g)(2), the words " ... such aggregate quantities as to substitute for a subscription to or purchase of such work" shall mean:
   (a) with respect to any given periodical (as opposed to any given issue of a periodical), filled requests of a library or archives (a "requesting entity") within any calendar year for a total of six or more copies of an article or articles published in such periodical within five years prior to the date of the request. These guidelines specifically shall not apply, directly or indirectly, to any request of a requesting entity for a copy or copies of an article or articles published in any issue of a periodical, the publication date of which is more than five years prior to the date when the request is made. The guidelines do not define the meaning, with respect to such a request, of " ... such aggregate quantities as to substitute for a subscription to (such periodical)."
   (b) with respect to any other material described in subsection 108(d), (including fiction and poetry), filled requests of a requesting entity within any calendar year for a total of six or more copies or phonorecords of or from any given work (including a collective work) during the entire period when such material shall be protected by copyright.

2. In the event that a requesting entity
   (a) shall have in force or shall have entered an order for a subscription to a periodical, or
   (b) has within its collection, or shall have entered an order for, a copy or phonorecord of any other copyrighted work, material from either category of which it desires to obtain by copy from another library or archives (the "sup-

plying entity"), because the material to be copied is not reasonably available for use by the requesting entity itself, then the fulfillment of such request shall be treated as though the requesting entity made such copy from its own collection. A library or archives may request a copy or phonorecord from a supplying entity only under those circumstances where the requesting entity would have been able, under the other provisions of section 108, to supply such copy from materials in its own collection.

3. No request for a copy or phonorecord of any material to which these guidelines apply may be fulfilled by the supplying entity unless such request is accompanied by a representation by the requesting entity that the request was made in conformity with these guidelines.

4. The requesting entity shall maintain records of all requests made by it for copies or phonorecords of any materials to which these guidelines apply and shall maintain records of the fulfillment of such requests, which records shall be retained until the end of the third complete calendar year after the end of the calendar year in which the respective request shall have been made.

5. As part of the review provided for in subsection 108(i), these guidelines shall be reviewed not later than five years from the effective date of this bill.

d. Conference Report: Discussion of "Audiovisual News Program"

The conference committee is aware that an issue has arisen as to the meaning of the phrase "audiovisual news program" in section 108(f) (3). The conferees believe that, under the provision as adopted in the conference substitute, a library or archives qualifying under section 108(a) would be free, without regard to the archival activities of the Library of Congress or any other organization, to reproduce, on videotape or any other medium of fixation or reproduction, local, regional, or network newscasts, interviews concerning current news events, and on-the-spot coverage of news events, and to distribute a limited number of reproductions of such a program on a loan basis.

e. Conference Report: Discussion of Libraries and Archives in Profit-Making Institutions

Another point of interpretation involves the meaning of "indirect commercial advantage," as used in section 108(a)(1), in the case of libraries or archival collections within industrial, profit-making, or proprietary institutions. As long as the library or archives meets the criteria in section 108(a) and the other requirements of the section, including the prohibitions against multiple and systematic copying in subsection (g), the conferees consider that the isolated, spontaneous making of single photocopies by a library or archives in a for-profit organization without any commercial motivation, or participation by such a library or archives in interlibrary arrangements, would come within the scope of section 108.

Appendix E:
Innocent Infringement by Library or Nonprofit Educational Institution

SECTION 504
INNOCENT INFRINGEMENT BY LIBRARY OR NONPROFIT EDUCATIONAL INSTITUTION

(a) **IN GENERAL.** Except as otherwise provided by this title, an infringer of copyright is liable for either—
　　(1) the copyright owner's actual damages and any additional profits of the infringer, as provided by subsection (b); or
　　(2) statutory damages, as provided by subsection (c).

(b) **Actual Damages and Profits.** The Copyright owner is entitled to recover the actual damages suffered by him or her as a result of the infringement, and any profits of the infringer that are attributable to the infringement and are not taken into account in computing the actual damages. In establishing the infringer's profits, the copyright owner is required to present proof only of the infringer's gross revenue, and the infringer is required to prove his or her deductible expenses and the elements of profit attributable to factors other than the copyrighted work.

(c) **Statutory Damages.**
   (1) Except as provided by clause (2) of this subsection, the Copyright owner may elect, at any time before final judgment is rendered, to recover, instead of actual damages and profits, an award of statutory damages for all infringements involved in the action, with respect to any one work, for which any one infringer is liable individually, or for which any two or more infringers are liable jointly and severally, in a sum of not less than $250 or more than $10,000 as the court considers just. For the purposes of this subsection, all the parts of a compilation or derivative work constitute one work.
   (2) In a case where the copyright owner sustains the burden of proving, and the court finds, that infringement was committed willfully, the court in its discretion may increase the award of statutory damages to a sum of not more than $50,000. In a case where the infringer sustains the burden of proving, and the court finds, that such infringer was not aware and had no reason to believe that his or her acts constituted an infringement of copyright, the court in its discretion may reduce the award of statutory damages to a sum of not less than $100. The court shall remit statutory damages in any case where an infringer believed and had reasonable ground that his or her use of the copyrighted work was a fair use under section 107, if the infringer was: (i) an employee or agent of a nonprofit educational institution, library, or archives acting within the scope of his or her employment who, or such institution, library, or archives itself, which infringed by reproducing the work in copies or phonorecords; or (ii) a public broadcasting entity which or a person who, as a regular part of the nonprofit activities of a public broadcasting entity (as defined in subsection (g) of section 118) infringed by performing a published nondramatic literary work or by reproducing a transmission program embodying a performance of such a work.

Appendix F:
Fair-Use Guidelines for Electronic Reserve Systems

Revised: March 5, 1996

INTRODUCTION

Many college, university, and school libraries have established reserve operations for readings and other materials that support the instructional requirements of specific courses. Some educational institutions are now providing electronic reserve systems that allow storage of electronic versions of materials that students may retrieve on a computer screen, and from which they may print a copy for their personal study. When materials are included as a matter of fair use, electronic reserve systems should constitute an ad hoc or supplemental source of information for students, beyond a textbook or other materials. If included with permission from the copyright owner, however, the scope and range of materials is potentially unlimited, depending upon the permission granted. Although fair use is determined on a case-by-case basis, the following guidelines identify an understanding of fair use for the reproduction, distribution, display, and performance of materials in the context of creating and using an electronic reserve system.

Making materials accessible through electronic reserve systems raises significant copyright issues. Electronic reserve operations include the making of a digital version of text, the distribution and display of that version at workstations, and downloading and printing of copies. The complexities of the electronic environment, and the growing potential for implicating copyright infringements, raise the need for a fresh understanding of fair use. These guidelines are not intended to burden the facilitation of reserves unduly, but instead offer a workable path that educators and librarians may follow in order to exercise a meaningful application of fair use, while also acknowledging and respecting the interests of copyright owners.

These guidelines focus generally on the traditional domain of reserve rooms, particularly copies of journal articles and book chapters, and their accompanying graphics. Nevertheless, they are not meant to apply exclusively to textual materials and may be instructive for the fair use of other media. The guidelines also focus on the use of the complete article or the entire book chapter. Using only brief excerpts from such works would most likely also be fair use, possibly without all of the restrictions or conditions set forth in these guidelines. Operators of reserve systems should also provide safeguards for the integrity of the text and the author's reputation, including verification that the text is correctly scanned.

The guidelines address only those materials protected by copyright and for which the institution has not obtained permission before including them in an electronic reserve system. The limitations and conditions set forth in these guidelines need not apply to materials in the public domain—such as works of the U.S. government or works on which copyright has expired—or to works for which the institution has obtained permission for inclusion in the electronic reserve system. License agreements may govern the uses of some materials. Persons responsible for electronic reserve systems should refer to applicable license terms for guidance. If an instructor arranges for students to acquire a work by some means that includes permission from the copyright owner, the instructor should not include that same work on an electronic reserve system as a matter of fair use.

These guidelines are the outgrowth of negotiations among diverse parties attending the Conference on Fair Use ("CONFU") meetings sponsored by the Information Infrastructure Task Force's Working Group on Intellectual Property Rights. While endorsements of any guidelines by all conference participants is unlikely, these guidelines have been endorsed by the organizations whose names appear at the end. These guidelines are in furtherance of the Working Group's objective of encouraging negotiated guidelines of fair use.

This introduction is an integral part of these guidelines and should be included with the guidelines wherever they may be reprinted or adopted by a library, academic institution, or other organization. No copyright protection of these guidelines is claimed by any person or entity, and anyone is free to reproduce and distribute this document without permission.

A. SCOPE OF MATERIAL

1. In accordance with fair use (Section 107 of the U.S. Copyright Act), electronic reserve systems may include copyrighted materials at the request of a course instructor.
2. Electronic reserve systems may include short items (such as an article from a journal, a chapter from a book or conference proceedings, or a poem from a collected work) or excerpts from longer items. "Longer items" may include articles, chapters, poems, and other works that are of such length as to constitute a substantial portion of a book, journal, or other work of which they may be a part. "Short items" may include articles, chapters, poems, and other works of a customary length and structure as to be a small part of a book, journal, or other work, even if that work may be marketed individually.
3. Electronic reserve systems should not include any material unless the instructor, the library, or another unit of the educational institution possesses a lawfully obtained copy.
4. The total amount of material included in electronic reserve systems for a specific course as a matter of fair use should be a small proportion of the total assigned reading for a particular course.

B. NOTICES AND ATTRIBUTIONS

1. On a preliminary or introductory screen, electronic reserve systems should display a notice, consistent with the notice described in Section 108(f)(1) of the Copyright Act. The notice should include additional language cautioning against further electronic distribution of the digital work.
2. If a notice of copyright appears on the copy of a work that is included in an electronic reserve system, the following

statement shall appear at some place where users will likely see it in connection with access to the particular work:

"The work from which this copy is made includes this notice: [restate the elements of the statutory copyright notice: e.g., Copyright 1996, XXX Corp.]"

3. Materials included in electronic reserve systems should include appropriate citations or attributions to their sources.

C. ACCESS AND USE

1. Electronic reserve systems should be structured to limit access to students registered in the course for which the items have been placed on reserve, and to instructors and staff responsible for the course or the electronic system.
2. The appropriate methods for limiting access will depend on available technology. Solely to suggest and not to prescribe options for implementation, possible methods for limiting access may include one or more of the following or other appropriate methods:
    (a) individual password controls or verification of a student's registration status; or
    (b) password system for each class; or
    (c) retrieval of works by course number or instructor name, but not by author or title of the work; or
    (d) access limited to workstations that are ordinarily used by, or are accessible to, only enrolled students or appropriate staff or faculty.
3. Students should not be charged specifically or directly for access to electronic reserve systems.

D. STORAGE AND REUSE

1. Permission from the copyright holder is required if the item is to be reused in a subsequent academic term for the same course offered by the same instructor, or if the item is a standard assigned or optional reading for an individual course taught in multiple sections by many instructors.
2. Material may be retained in electronic form while permission is being sought or until the next academic term in

which the material might be used, but in no event for more than three calendar years, including the year in which the materials are last used.

3. Short-term access to materials included on electronic reserve systems in previous academic terms may be provided to students who have not completed the course.

Appendix G:
Intellectual Property:
An Association of Research
Libraries Statement of
Principles

"The primary objective of copyright is not to reward the labor of authors, but [t]o promote the Progress of Science and useful Arts. To this end, copyright assures authors the right to their original expression, but encourages others to build freely upon the ideas and information conveyed by a work. This result is neither unfair nor unfortunate. It is the means by which copyright advances the progress of science and art."

— Justice Sandra Day O'Connor

AFFIRMING THE RIGHTS AND RESPONSIBILITIES OF THE RESEARCH LIBRARY COMMUNITY IN THE AREA OF COPYRIGHT

The genius of United States copyright law is that it balances the intellectual property rights of authors, publishers and copyright owners with society's need for the free exchange of ideas. Taken together, fair use and other public rights to utilize copyrighted works, as established in the Copyright Act of 1976, constitute indispensable legal doctrines for promoting the dissemination of knowledge, while ensuring authors, publishers and copyright owners protection of their creative works and economic investments. The preservation and continuation of these balanced rights in an electronic environment are essential to the free flow of information and to the development of an information infrastructure that serves the public interest.

The U.S. and Canada have adopted very different approaches to intellectual property and copyright issues. For example, the Canadian Copyright Act does not contain the special considerations for library and educational use found in the U.S. Copyright Act of 1976, nor does it place federal or provincial government works in the public domain. Because of these differences, this statement addresses these issues from the U.S. perspective.

Each year, millions of researchers, students, and members of the public benefit from access to library collections - access that is supported by fair use, the right of libraries to reproduce materials under certain circumstances, and other related provisions of the copyright law. These provisions are limitations on the rights of copyright owners. The loss of these provisions in the emerging information infrastructure would greatly harm scholarship, teaching, and the operations of a free society. Fair use, the library and other relevant provisions must be preserved so that copyright ownership does not become an absolute monopoly over the distribution of and access to copyrighted information. In an electronic environment, this could mean that information resources are accessible only to those who are able to pay. The public information systems that libraries have developed would be replaced by commercial information vendors. In the age of information, a diminished scope of public rights would lead to an increasingly polarized society of information haves and have-nots.

Librarians and educators have every reason to encourage full and good-faith copyright compliance. Technological advancement has made copyright infringement easier to accomplish, but no less illegal. Authors, publishers, copyright owners, and librarians are integral parts of the system of scholarly communication and publishers, authors, and copyright owners are the natural partners of education and research. The continuation of fair use, the library and other relevant provisions of the Copyright Act of 1976 applied in an electronic environment offer the prospect of better library services, better teaching, and better research, without impairing the market for copyrighted materials.

Although the emerging information infrastructure is raising awareness of technological changes that pose challenges to copyright systems, the potential impact of technology was anticipated by the passage of the Copyright Act of 1976. Congress expressly intended that the revised copyright law would apply to all types of media. With few exceptions, the protections and provisions of the copyright statute are as relevant and applicable to an electronic environment as they are to a print and broadcast environment.

The research library community believes that the development of an information infrastructure does not require a major revision of copyright law at this time. In general, the stakeholders affected by intellectual property law continue to be well served by the existing copyright statute. Just as was intended, the law's flexibility with regard to dissemination media fosters change and experimentation in educational and research communication. Some specific legislative changes may be needed to ensure that libraries are able to utilize the latest technology to provide continued and effective access to information and to preserve knowledge.

The Association of Research Libraries affirms the following intellectual property principles as they apply to librarians, teachers, researchers, and other information mediators and consumers. We join our national leaders in the determination to develop a policy framework for the emerging information infrastructure that strengthens the Constitutional purpose of copyright law to advance science and the useful arts.

STATEMENT OF PRINCIPLES

Principle 1: Copyright exists for the public good.

The United States copyright law is founded on a Constitutional provision intended to "promote the progress of Science and Useful Arts." The fundamental purpose of copyright is to serve the public interest by encouraging the advancement of knowledge through a system of exclusive but limited rights for authors and copyright owners. Fair use and other public rights to utilize copyrighted works, specifically and intentionally included in the 1976 revision of the law, provide the essential balance between the rights of authors, publishers and copyright owners, and society's interest in the free exchange of ideas.

Principle 2: Fair use, the library, and other relevant provisions of the Copyright Act of 1976 must be preserved in the development of the emerging information infrastructure.

Fair use and other relevant provisions are the essential means by which teachers teach, students learn, and researchers advance knowledge. The Copyright Act of 1976 defines intellectual property principles in a way that is independent of the form of publication or distribution. These provisions apply to all formats and are essential to modern library and information services.

Principle 3: As trustees of the rapidly growing record of human knowledge, libraries and archives must have full use of technology in order to preserve our heritage of scholarship and research.

Digital works of enduring value need to be preserved just as printed works have long been preserved by research libraries. Archival responsibilities have traditionally been undertaken by libraries because publishers and database producers have generally preserved particular knowledge only as long as it has economic value in the marketplace. As with other formats, the preservation of electronic information will be the responsibility of libraries and they will continue to perform this important societal role.

The policy framework of the emerging information infrastructure must provide for the archiving of electronic materials by research libraries to maintain permanent collections and environments for public access. Accomplishing this goal will require strengthening the library provisions of the copyright law to allow preservation activities which use electronic or other appropriate technologies as they emerge.

Principle 4: Licensing agreements should not be allowed to abrogate the fair use and library provisions authorized in the copyright statute.

Licenses may define the rights and privileges of the contracting parties differently than those defined by the Copyright Act of 1976. But licenses and contracts should not negate fair use and the public right to utilize copyrighted works. The research library community recognizes that there will be a variety of payment methods for the purchase of copyrighted materials in electronic formats, just as there are differing contractual agreements for acquiring printed information. The research library community is committed to working with publishers and database producers to develop model agreements that deploy licenses that do not contract around fair use or other copyright provisions.

Principle 5: Librarians and educators have an obligation to educate information users about their rights and responsibilities under intellectual property law.

Institutions of learning must continue to employ policies and procedures that encourage copyright compliance. For example, the Copyright Act of 1976 required the posting of copyright notices on photocopy equipment. This practice should be updated to other technologies which permit the duplication of copyrighted works.

Principle 6: Copyright should not be applied to U.S. government information.

The Copyright Act of 1976 prohibits copyright of U.S. government works. Only under selected circumstances has Congress granted limited exceptions to this policy. The Copyright Act of 1976 is one of several laws that support a fundamental principle of democratic government—that the open exchange of public information is essential to the functioning of a free and open society. U.S. government information should remain in the public domain free of copyright or copyright-like restrictions.

Principle 7: The information infrastructure must permit authors to be compensated for the success of their creative works, and copyright owners must have an opportunity for a fair return on their investment.

The research library community affirms that the distribution of copyrighted information which exceeds fair use and the enumerated limitations of the law require the permission of and/or compensation to authors, publishers and copyright owners. The continuation of library provisions and fair use in an electronic environment has far greater potential to promote the sale of copyrighted materials than to substitute for purchase. There is every reason to believe that the increasing demand for and use of copyrighted works fostered by new information technologies will result in the equivalent or even greater compensation for authors, publishers and copyright owners. The information infrastructure however, must be based on an underlying ethos of abundance rather than scarcity. With such an approach, authors, copyright owners, and publishers will have a full range of new opportunities in an electronic information environment and libraries will be able to perform their roles as partners in promoting science and the useful arts.

Adopted by the ARL Membership
May 1994

Index

Colophon

Arlene Bielefield is currently on the faculty of the Department of Library Science and Instructional Technology at Southern Connecticut State University (SCSU) in New Haven, Connecticut. Arlene holds a Juris Doctor from the University of Connecticut School of Law, having graduated and passed the Connecticut Bar in 1981. She also holds a Masters in Library Science degree from SCSU.

In 1994, Arlene authored *Legally Effective Corporate Communication* for Panel Books. She is presently working, with Judge John J. Daly, on a revised edition of Holden and Daly's *Connecticut Evidence*.

A past president of the Connecticut Library Association, Arlene has served on a number of professional committees. She is increasingly in demand as a speaker on copyright.

Lawrence Cheeseman holds an M.S. in Library and Information Science from Pratt Institute as well as a graduate and undergraduate degree in philosophy and the history of science. He has been a practicing law librarian for 29 years including several years as chief law librarian with a law firm specializing in intellectual property law. He is currently supervising a group of 7 public law libraries. He has also co-authored *Maintaining the Privacy of Library Records: A Handbook and Guide* and the *Connecticut Legal Research Handbook*.

In 1992, Arlene and co-author Lawrence Cheeseman wrote the *Connecticut Legal Research Guide* for the Connecticut Law Book Company.

In 1993, Arlene and Larry wrote their first copyright book *(Libraries & Copyright Law)*, the introductory volume in a series on Libraries & the Law for Neal-Schuman Publishers. Next came *Library Employment and the Law* (1993), *Maintaining the Privacy of Library Records* (1994), *and Library Patrons & the Law* (1995).

TECHNOLOGY AND COPYRIGHT LAW
A Guidebook for the Library, Research, and Teaching Professions

1999 Update

Arlene Bielefield
and
Lawrence Cheeseman

Neal-Schuman Publishers, Inc.

New York   London

Since 1997, when *Technology and Copyright Law: A Guidebook for the Library, Research, and Teaching Professions* was published, the passage of new legislation has contributed to the understanding and refinement of copyright protection in an electronic medium. Neal-Schuman has published this update in conjunction with *Technology and Copyright Law* to help librarians, researchers, and teachers comply with and take advantage of this recent copyright legislation.

1999 Update to
Technology and Copyright Law

Contents

Laws Update

NO ELECTRONIC THEFT (NET) ACT[1]

In 1997 Congress directly responded to a Federal District Court decision[2] concerning the posting of copyrighted programs on an electronic bulletin board. Since no commercial advantage or private financial gain was realized, the District Court ruled that the defendant could not be prosecuted for piracy of copyrighted works. NET redefines "financial gain" in the criminal statute to include: "receipt, or expectation of receipt, of anything of value, including the receipt of other copyrighted works." While this act does not affect innocent infringement by library or nonprofit educational institutions (section 504), it does establish a new de minimis for criminal willful infringement of copyright.[3]

DIGITAL MILLENNIUM COPYRIGHT ACT (DMCA)[4]

In 1998 Congress passed DMCA to make it possible for the United States to join two World Intellectual Property Organization treaties concluded in Geneva in December of 1996,[5] and to update the copyright law to deal with new technologies. Thanks to efforts of library groups, however, DMCA does not include the Collections of Information Antipiracy Act (S. 2291/H.R. 2652), which would have extended copyright protection for the first time to facts.

Copyright Protection Measures

DMCA adds a new chapter—Chapter 12—to the copyright law (title 17 of the United States Code) that prohibits the circumvention of technical copyright protection measures. (e.g. a password or form of encription used by a copyright holder to restrict access to its material).[6] There are two limitations on this prohibition. First, an exemption allows nonprofit libraries, archives, or education institutions to circumvent copyright protection systems to determine if it wishes to acquire a copy.[7] Second and most significant, Chapter 12 contains provisions preserving fair use after a user has gained authorized access to a work because it distinguishes between access-prevention technology and infringement-prevention technology, and:

> As a result, an individual would not be able to circumvent in order to gain unauthorized access to a work, but would be able to do so in order to make fair use of a work which she has lawfully acquired.[8]

The text provisions of Chapter 12 relating to libraries appear below:

CHAPTER 12—COPYRIGHT PROTECTION AND MANAGEMENT SYSTEMS

Sec. 1201. Circumvention of copyright protection systems

*　　*　　*　　*

(c) OTHER RIGHTS, ETC., NOT AFFECTED- (1) Nothing in this section shall affect rights, remedies, limitations, or defenses to copyright infringement, including fair use, under this title.

(d) EXEMPTION FOR NONPROFIT LIBRARIES, ARCHIVES, AND EDUCATIONAL INSTITUTIONS- (1) A nonprofit library, archives, or educational institution which gains access to a commercially exploited copyrighted work solely in order to make a good faith determination of whether to acquire a copy of that work for the sole purpose of engaging in conduct permitted under this title shall not be in violation of subsection (a)(1)(A). A copy of a work to which access has been gained under this paragraph—

(A) may not be retained longer than necessary to make such good faith determination; and

(B) may not be used for any other purpose.

(2) The exemption made available under paragraph (1) shall only apply with respect to a work when an identical copy of that work is not reasonably available in another form.

(3) A nonprofit library, archives, or educational institution that willfully for the purpose of commercial advantage or financial gain violates paragraph (1)—

(A) shall, for the first offense, be subject to the civil remedies under section 1203; and

(B) shall, for repeated or subsequent offenses, in addition to the civil remedies under section 1203, forfeit the exemption provided under paragraph (1).

(4) This subsection may not be used as a defense to a claim under subsection (a)(2) or (b), nor may this subsection permit a nonprofit library, archives, or educational institution to manufacture, import, offer to the public, provide, or otherwise traffic in any technology, product, service, component, or part thereof, which circumvents a technological measure.

(5) In order for a library or archives to qualify for the exemption under this subsection, the collections of that library or archives shall be—

(A) open to the public; or

(B) available not only to researchers affiliated with the library or archives or with the institution of which it is a part, but also to other persons doing research in a specialized field.

*   *   *   *   *   *

Sec. 1203. Civil remedies

*   *   *   *   *   *   *

(c) AWARD OF DAMAGES

*   *   *   *   *

(5) Innocent violations

NONPROFIT LIBRARY, ARCHIVES, OR EDUCATIONAL INSTITU-TIONS—In the case of a nonprofit library, archives, or educational institution, the court shall remit damages in any case in which the library, archives, or educational institution sustains the burden of proving, and the court finds, that the library, archives, or educational institution was not aware and had no reason to believe that its acts constituted a violation.

Sec. 1204. Criminal offenses and penalties

*   *   *   *   *

(b) LIMITATION FOR NONPROFIT LIBRARY, ARCHIVES, OR EDUCA-TIONAL INSTITUTION- Subsection (a) shall not apply to a nonprofit library, archives, or educational institution

*   *   *   *   *

Sec. 404. Exemption for Libraries and Archives.

Section 108 of title 17, United States Code, is amended—

(2) in subsection (b)

(A) by striking 'a copy or phonorecord' and inserting 'three copies or phonorecords';

(B) by striking 'in facsimile form'; and

(C) by striking 'if the copy or phonorecord reproduced is currently in the collections of the library or archives.' and inserting 'if—

'(1) the copy or phonorecord reproduced is currently in the collections of the library or archives; and

'(2) any such copy or phonorecord that is reproduced in digital format is not otherwise distributed in that format and is not made available to the public in that format outside the premises of the library or archives.'; and

(3) in subsection (c)—

(A) by striking 'a copy or phonorecord' and inserting 'three copies or phonorecords';

(B) by striking 'in facsimile form';

(C) by inserting 'or if the existing format in which the work is stored has become obsolete,' after 'stolen,';

(D) by striking 'if the library or archives has, after a reasonable effort, determined that an unused replacement cannot be obtained at a fair price.' and inserting 'if—

'(1) the library or archives has, after a reasonable effort, determined that an unused replacement cannot be obtained at a fair price; and

'(2) any such copy or phonorecord that is reproduced in digital format is not made available to the public in that format outside the premises of the library or archives in lawful possession of such copy.'; and

(E) by adding at the end the following:

'For purposes of this subsection, a format shall be considered obsolete if the machine or device necessary to render perceptible a work stored in that format is no longer manufactured or is no longer reasonably available in the commercial marketplace.'

DMCA, Distance Learning, Section 403

In the fast-growing field of distance education, questions concerning copyright abound. What copyrighted works and technologies may a teacher or professor use in the electronic classroom? Can the Fair Use Guidelines for Classroom Copying or for the Educational Use of Music be the basis for the use of digital technologies in a distance education format? Are these established guidelines usable in some distance education formats and not others? Is it possible to establish one set of guidelines for all distance education formats, from the two-way audio and video systems that emulate the traditional classroom to the courses taught completely via the Internet? These and other questions require answers as quickly as possible.

Realizing the need for answers and recognizing that the Conference on Fair Use (CONFU) participants expended two-and-a-half years trying, without success, to agree on fair use guidelines for a variety of new technologies, Congress incorporated a process and timeline in the Digital Millenium Copyright Act to deal with these copyright issues.

Section 403 of the Digital Millenium Copyright Act requires that the Copyright Office consult with various constituencies to formulate recommendations to Congress on "how to promote distance education through digital technologies...while maintaining an appropriate balance between the rights of copyright owners and the interests of users." To that end, the Copyright Office has published notice in the *Federal Register* seeking interested parties and setting up a schedule for comments and hearings. The Copyright Office Web site at <www.lcweb.loc.gov/copyright/disted/> provides access to this material and other information of interest to those in the library, research, and teaching professions.

The Copyright Office Web site includes the following information:

COPYRIGHT OFFICE STUDY ON DISTANCE EDUCATION

- Text Links
  Section 403 of the Digital Millennium Copyright Act (version: pdf)
  Federal Register Notice Seeking Identification of Interested Parties
  Federal Register Notice Seeking Written Comments (version: pdf)

- Background
  On October 28, 1998, H.R. 2281, the Digital Millennium Copyright Act, was enacted into law. Section 403 requires that the Copyright Office consult with representatives of copyright owners, nonprofit educational institutions, and nonprofit libraries and archives, and thereafter submit to Congress recommendations on how to promote distance education through digital technologies, including interactive digital networks, while maintaining an appropriate balance between the rights of copyright owners and the interests of users. Such recommendations may include legislative changes. Section 403 requires the Copyright Office to submit its recommendations to Congress no later than April 28, 1999.

- About this page
  The Copyright Office will post copies of all public notices, written comments, and other material relevant to the distance education study on this Web page as it becomes available. The Office's Report will be posted here as well.

- Important dates

October 28, 1998	Digital Millennium Copyright Act enacted.
November 16, 1998	Date of Federal Register notice requesting identification of interested parties.
December 7, 1998	Due date for responses to November 16 *Federal Register* notice requesting identification of interested parties.
December 23, 1998	Date of *Federal Register* notice seeking written comments and testimony.
January 12, 1999	Due date for all requests to testify at public hearings.
January 15, 1999	Due date for summaries of oral testimony for Washington, DC public hearing.
January 25, 1999	Distance education demonstration at Library of Congress.
January 26–27, 1999	Washington, DC public hearing.
February 1, 1999	Due date for summaries of oral testimony for Los Angeles, CA public hearing.
February 2, 1999	Due date for summaries of oral testimony for Chicago, IL public hearing.
February 5, 1999	All written comments due.
February 10, 1999	Los Angeles, CA public hearing.
February 12, 1999	Chicago, IL public hearing.
March 3, 1999	All reply comments due.
April 28, 1999	Copyright Office recommendations due to Congress.

- Questions?
  Please note that the electronic mail address disted@loc.gov exists for the sole purpose of accepting written statements in response to the *Federal Register* notice published at 63 FR 71167 on December 23, 1998.
  If you have questions regarding the Copyright Office Study on the Promotion of Distance Education through Digital Technologies please contact Sayuri Rajapakse, Attorney-Advisor, by telephone at 202–707–8350, by fax at 202–707–8366, or by electronic mail at ssra@loc.gov.

Sonny Bono Copyright Term Extension Act, Title I, and Interim Regulations Regarding Notice to Libraries and Archives

SUMMARY

Effective October 27, 1998 the Sonny Bono Copyright Term Extension Act, Public Law 105–298, essentially added 20 years to the period of copyright protection. Title I of the Act is printed below. Those wishing to view the Act in its entirety, including the path of the bill (S. 505), sponsors, and other information, can find it at the Thomas location: <thomas.loc.gov>.

A brief summary of the major extension-of-term provisions are as follows:

For works created after January 1, 1978:
1. Copyright protection extends for the life of the author plus 70 years;
2. For joint works, copyright protection extends for 70 years after the death of the last surviving author;
3. For anonymous or pseudonymous works, or for works made for hire, protection exists for 95 years from the year of first publi-

cation or 120 years from the year of creation, whichever expires first.

For works created but not published or registered before January 1, 1978:
1. Copyright protection extends for the life of the author plus 70 years, but in no case will it expire earlier than December 31, 2002;
2. If a work is published before December 31, 2002, the term will not expire before December 31, 2047.

For pre-1978 works still in their original or renewal term of copyright
1. The total term is extended to 95 years from the date that copyright was originally secured.

There are additional provisions concerning sound recordings made before February 15, 1972; termination of grants and licenses; and presumption of an author's death. For information about these provisions, call the Public Information Office of the Copyright Office at (202)707–3000, Monday through Friday, 8:30 a.m.-5 p.m., eastern time.   Libraries, archives, and nonprofit educational institutions have an exception under the law that permits them to treat a copyrighted work in its last 20 years of protection as if it were in the public domain for noncommercial purposes. But this exception applies only if 1) a good faith investigation shows that the work is "not subject to commercial exploitation," and 2) use of the work stops if the copyright owner provides notice to the contrary.

INTERIM REGULATIONS

Interim regulations have been developed by the Copyright Office in regard to **Notice to Libraries and Archives of Normal Commercial Exploitation or Availability at Reasonable Price.** These regulations may be found in the *Code of Federal Regulations* at 37 CFR 201 and at the Copyright Office Web site at <lcweb. loc.gov/copyright/>. The summary portion of the regulations states:

> SUMMARY: The Copyright Office of the Library of Congress is issuing interim regulations and requesting comment on the requirements by which a copyright owner or its agent may provide notice to libraries and

archives that a published work in the final 20 years of its extended term of copyright is subject to normal commercial exploitation or that a copy or phonorecord of the work can be obtained at a reasonable price. The Office is issuing interim regulations in order to have the notice requirements in place on January 1, 1999. Final regulations will be promulgated following the Office's review of public comments.

The body of the regulations contains this information of interest to libraries:

> Under the interim regulations set forth at 37 CFR 201.39, copyright owners may file with the Copyright Office a Notice to Libraries and Archives of Normal Commercial Exploitation or Availability at Reasonable Price. The Notice shall be accompanied by a filing fee of $50 for the first work, and $20 for each additional work, made payable in check, money order or bank draft to the Register of Copyrights. The Office will not provide printed forms for the Notices, but will provide a required format, which is set out in Appendix A to this notice and will be available from the Copyright Office website (lcweb.loc.gov/copyright). The regulations specify that the Notice must be provided on 8 1/2 x 11 inch paper with a one-inch margin.
>
> Copyright owners or their agents may file the Notice at any time during the work's extended 20–year term, and thereafter a library or archives could not claim the exemption with respect to the identified work. Until such notice is filed, however, a library or archive is free to use a published work in its last 20 years of copyright term as provided under section 108(h) unless its reasonable investigation otherwise reveals that the work is subject to normal commercial exploitation or availability at a reasonable price. The Office is inquiring whether the final regulations should permit copyright owners to file a Notice for a work before its extended term begins and, if so, how much sooner.

The regulations—spanning eight pages of single-spaced type in the *Federal Register* Online—also contain background information, a listing of fees for different types of notification to libraries and archives, the elements necessary for notification, and seven categories of questions for public comment.

**SONNY BONO COPYRIGHT TERM EXTENSION ACT, TITLE I
(PUBLIC LAW 105–298)
S.505
One Hundred Fifth Congress of the United States of America
AT THE SECOND SESSION
Begun and held at the City of Washington on Tuesday,
the twenty-seventh day of January, one thousand nine hundred
and ninety-eight**

An Act To amend the provisions of title 17, United States Code, with respect to the duration of copyright, and for other purposes.
Be it enacted by the Senate and House of Representatives of the United States of America in Congress assembled,

TITLE I—COPYRIGHT TERM EXTENSION

SEC. 101. SHORT TITLE.

This title may be referred to as the 'Sonny Bono Copyright Term Extension Act'.

SEC. 102. DURATION OF COPYRIGHT PROVISIONS.

(a) PREEMPTION WITH RESPECT TO OTHER LAWS- Section 301(c) of title 17, United States Code, is amended by striking 'February 15, 2047' each place it appears and inserting 'February 15, 2067'.
(b) DURATION OF COPYRIGHT: WORKS CREATED ON OR AFTER JANU-ARY 1, 1978- Section 302 of title 17, United States Code, is amended—
    (1) in subsection (a) by striking 'fifty' and inserting '70';
    (2) in subsection (b) by striking 'fifty' and inserting '70';
    (3) in subsection (c) in the first sentence—
        (A) by striking 'seventy-five' and inserting '95'; and
        (B) by striking 'one hundred' and inserting '120'; and
    (4) in subsection (e) in the first sentence—
        (A) by striking 'seventy-five' and inserting '95';
        (B) by striking 'one hundred' and inserting '120'; and
        (C) by striking 'fifty' each place it appears and inserting '70'.
(c) DURATION OF COPYRIGHT: WORKS CREATED BUT NOT PUBLISHED OR COPYRIGHTED
BEFORE JANUARY 1, 1978- Section 303 of title 17, United States Code, is amended in the second sentence by striking 'December 31, 2027' and inserting 'December 31, 2047'.
(d) DURATION OF COPYRIGHT: SUBSISTING COPYRIGHTS-
    (1) IN GENERAL- Section 304 of title 17, United States Code, is amended—
        (A) in subsection (a)—

(i) in paragraph (1)—

(I) in subparagraph (B) by striking '47' and inserting '67';

and

(II) in subparagraph (C) by striking '47' and inserting '67';

(ii) in paragraph (2)—

(I) in subparagraph (A) by striking '47' and inserting '67';

and

(II) in subparagraph (B) by striking '47' and inserting '67';

and

(iii) in paragraph (3)—

(I) in subparagraph (A)(i) by striking '47' and inserting '67';

and

(II) in subparagraph (B) by striking '47' and inserting '67';

(B) by amending subsection (b) to read as follows:

'(b) COPYRIGHTS IN THEIR RENEWAL TERM AT THE TIME OF THE EF-FECTIVE DATE OF THE SONNY BONO COPYRIGHT TERM EXTENSION ACT—Any copyright still in its renewal term at the time that the Sonny Bono Copyright Term Extension Act becomes effective shall have a copyright term of 95 years from the date copyright was originally secured.';

(C) in subsection (c)(4)(A) in the first sentence by inserting 'or, in the case of a termination under subsection (d), within the five-year period specified by subsection (d)(2),' after 'specified by clause (3) of this subsection,'; and

(D) by adding at the end the following new subsection:

'(d) TERMINATION RIGHTS PROVIDED IN SUBSECTION (c) WHICH HAVE EXPIRED ON OR BEFORE THE EFFECTIVE DATE OF THE SONNY BONO COPYRIGHT TERM EXTENSION ACT-In

the case of any copyright other than a work made for hire, subsisting in its renewal term on the effective date of the Sonny Bono Copyright Term Extension Act for which the termination right provided in subsection (c) has expired by such date, where the author or owner of the termination right has not previously exercised such termination right, the exclusive or nonexclusive grant of a transfer or license of the renewal copyright or any right under it, executed before January 1, 1978, by any of the persons designated in subsection (a)(1)(C) of this section, other than by will, is subject to termination under the following conditions:

'(1) The conditions specified in subsections (c) (1), (2), (4), (5), and (6) of this section apply to terminations of the last 20 years of copyright term as provided by the amendments made by the Sonny Bono Copyright Term Extension Act.

'(2) Termination of the grant may be effected at any time during a period of 5 years beginning at the end of 75 years from the date copyright was originally secured.'.

(2) COPYRIGHT AMENDMENTS ACT OF 1992– Section 102 of the Copyright Amendments Act of 1992 (Public Law 102–307; 106 Stat. 266; 17 U.S.C. 304 note) is amended—

    (A) in subsection (c)—

        (i) by striking '47' and inserting '67';

        (ii) by striking '(as amended by subsection (a) of this section)'; and

        (iii) by striking 'effective date of this section' each place it appears and inserting 'effective date of the Sonny Bono Copyright Term Extension Act'; and

    (B) in subsection (g)(2) in the second sentence by inserting before the period the following: 'except each reference to forty-seven years in such provisions shall be deemed to be 67 years'.

SEC. 103. TERMINATION OF TRANSFERS AND LICENSES COVERING EXTENDED RENEWAL TERM.

Sections 203(a)(2) and 304(c)(2) of title 17, United States Code, are each amended—

    (1) by striking 'by his widow or her widower and his or her children or grandchildren'; and

    (2) by inserting after subparagraph (C) the following:

        '(D) In the event that the author's widow or widower, children, and grandchildren are not living, the author's executor, administrator, personal representative, or trustee shall own the author's entire termination interest.'.

SEC. 104. REPRODUCTION BY LIBRARIES AND ARCHIVES.

    Section 108 of title 17, United States Code, is amended—

    (1) by redesignating subsection (h) as subsection (i); and

    (2) by inserting after subsection (g) the following:

'(h)(1) For purposes of this section, during the last 20 years of any term of copyright of a published work, a library or archives, including a non-profit educational institution that functions as such, may reproduce, distribute, display, or perform in facsimile or digital form a copy or phonorecord of such work, or portions thereof, for purposes of preservation, scholarship, or research, if such library or archives has first determined, on the basis of a reasonable investigation, that none of the conditions set forth in subparagraphs (A), (B), and (C) of paragraph (2) apply.

    '(2) No reproduction, distribution, display, or performance is authorized under this subsection if—

        '(A) the work is subject to normal commercial exploitation;

        '(B) a copy or phonorecord of the work can be obtained at a reasonable price; or

'(C) the copyright owner or its agent provides notice pursuant to regulations promulgated by the Register of Copyrights that either of the conditions set forth in subparagraphs (A) and (B) applies.

'(3) The exemption provided in this subsection does not apply to any subsequent uses by users other than such library or archives.'

SEC. 105. VOLUNTARY NEGOTIATION REGARDING DIVISION OF ROYALTIES.

It is the sense of the Congress that copyright owners of audiovisual works for which the term of copyright protection is extended by the amendments made by this title, and the screenwriters, directors, and performers of those audiovisual works, should negotiate in good faith in an effort to reach a voluntary agreement or voluntary agreements with respect to the establishment of a fund or other mechanism for the amount of remuneration to be divided among the parties for the exploitation of those audiovisual works.

SEC. 106. EFFECTIVE DATE.

This title and the amendments made by this title shall take effect on the date of the enactment of this Act.

PROPOSED COPYRIGHT OFFICE FEE SCHEDULE SENT TO CONGRESS FEBRUARY 1, 1999

New statutory fees for Congressional approval § 708 (a) (1)-9)	Proposed fee
Registration of a claim in literary materials other than serials (Form TX)	$30
Registration of a claim in a serial (Form SE)	$30
Registration of a claim in a work of the performing arts, including sound recordings and audiovisual works (Form PA, Form SR)	$30
Registration of a claim in a work of the visual arts (Form VA)	$30
Registration in a claim in GRCP (group of contributions to periodicals)	$30
Registration of a renew	
• Claim without Addendum (Form RE)	$45
• Claim with Addendum (Form RE)	$60
Registration of a correction or amplification to a claim (Form CA)	$65
Providing an additional certificate of registration	$25
Any other certification (per hour)	$65
Search—report prepared from official records (per hour)	$65
Search—locating Copyright Office records (per hour)	$65
Recordation of document (single title)	$50
• Additional titles (per group of 10 titles)	$15

ANNOUNCEMENT OF NEW SPECIAL FEES §708 (A)(10) EFFECTIVE JULY 1, 1999

Registration of a claim in a group of serials (Form SE/Group)	$10/issue— $30 minimum
Registration of a claim in a group of daily newspapers, including qualified newsletters (Form G/DN)	$55
Registration of a restored copyright (Form GATT)	$30
Registration of a claim in a group of restored works (Form GATT/Group)	$10/claim— $30 minimum

Cases Update

On April 9, 1996, the U.S. Court of Appeals, 6th Circuit, ordered that its previous decision *Princeton University Press v. Michigan Document Services, Inc.* be vacated (see p. 66–68. The case was about reproduction of excerpts to be used in coursepacks for students, similar to the Kinko's case).[9] On November 4, 1998, The U.S. Court of Appeals for the 2nd Circuit ruled in *Matthew Bender Co. v. West Publishing Co.* had no copyright to the pagination in its published court decisions.[10] (This case concerned public domain material that had been republished. The publisher wanted to copyright the entire publication, including public domain material and page numbers.) The decision was contrary to a previous decision of the U.S. Court of Appeals for the 8th Circuit.[11]

Update on Guidelines for Fair Use in Nonprofit Educational Institutions

The early fair use guidelines generated prior to January 1, 1978, when the present copyright law [Copyright Act of 1976] went into effect, have stood the test of time and are still considered a "safe harbor." However, because of the perceived need to deal with new technologies, the Conference on Fair Use (CONFU), an offshoot of the National Information Infrastructure task force convened in 1994 by the then Secretary of Commerce, Ron Brown, attempted to generate a series of fair use guidelines for various electronic formats—for example, digital imaging, electronic reserves, electronic interlibrary loan, distance learning, use and production of multimedia. By 1997, it was clear that the CONFU draft documents for these proposed guidelines had failed to achieve sufficient endorsement to ensure their survival.

Meanwhile the Consortium of College and University Media Centers (CCUMC) developed a draft of Fair Use Guidelines for Educational Multimedia (dated July 1996). These guidelines, like those already in place for classroom copying, etc., are not part of the law. What they represent is an agreement among the endorsers about the limits of fair use in a particular medium at a particular time. Since these guidelines are untested in the courts, they cannot be considered a "safe harbor" at this time. However, since they have been endorsed by both a number of publishers and users of copyrighted materials, they have been described as having a life of their own. Notice should be given to the fact that none of the major library associations has endorsed them.

While we have included The Fair Use Guidelines for Educational Multimedia from the URL listed below here, readers may wish to access them for the latest updates and information at <www_ninch.cni.org/ISSUES/COPYRIGHT/FAIR_USE_EDUCA TION/CONFU/multimedia>

FAIR USE GUIDELINES FOR EDUCATIONAL MULTIMEDIA[1]

TABLE OF CONTENTS (printed from ninch.cni.org site on February 20, 1999)

1. INTRODUCTION
1.1 Preamble

Fair use is a legal principle that defines the limitations on the exclusive rights of copyright holders[2]. The purpose of these guidelines is to provide guidance on the application of fair use principles by educators, scholars and students who develop multimedia projects using portions of copyrighted works under fair use rather than by seeking authorization for non-commercial educational uses. These guidelines apply only to fair use in the context of copyright and to no other rights.

There is no simple test to determine what is fair use. Section 107 of the Copyright Act[3] sets forth the four fair use factors which should be considered in each instance, based on the particular facts of a given case, to determine whether a use is a "fair use": (1) the purpose and character of the use, including whether use is of a commercial nature or is for nonprofit educational purposes, (2) the nature of the copyrighted work, (3) the amount and substantiality of the portion used in relation to the copyrighted work as a whole, and (4) the effect of the use upon the potential market for or value of the copyrighted work.

While only the courts can authoritatively determine whether a particular use is fair use, these guidelines represent the participants'[4] consensus of conditions under which fair use should generally apply and examples of when permission is required. Uses that exceed these guidelines may or may not be fair use. The participants also agree that the more one exceeds these guidelines, the greater the risk that fair use does not apply.

The limitations and conditions set forth in these guidelines do not apply to works in the public domain—such as U.S. Government works or works on which copyright has expired for which there are no copyright restrictions—or to works for which the individual or institution has obtained permission for the particular use. Also, license agreements may govern the uses of some works and users should refer to the applicable license terms for guidance.

The participants who developed these guidelines met for an extended period of time and the result represents their collective understanding in this complex area. Because digital technology is in a dynamic phase, there may come a time when it is necessary to review the guidelines. Nothing in these guidelines shall be construed to apply to the fair use privilege in any context outside of educational and scholarly uses of educational multimedia projects.

This Preamble is an integral part of these guidelines and should be included whenever the guidelines are reprinted or adopted by organizations and educational institutions. Users are encouraged to reproduce and distribute these guidelines freely without permission; no copyright protection of these guidelines is claimed by any person or entity.

[1] These Guidelines shall not be read to supersede other preexisting education fair use guidelines that deal with the Copyright Act of 1976.

[2] See Section 106 of the Copyright Act.

[3] The Copyright Act of 1976, as amended, is codified as 17 U.S.C. Sec.101 et seq.

[4] The names of the various organizations participating in this dialog appear at the end of these guidelines and clearly indicate the variety of interest groups involved, both from the standpoint of the users of copyrighted material and also from the standpoint of the copyright owners.

1.2 Background

These guidelines clarify the application of fair use of copyrighted works as teaching methods are adapted to new learning environments. Educators have traditionally brought copyrighted books, videos, slides, sound recordings and other media into the classroom, along with accompanying projection and playback equipment. Multimedia creators integrated these individual instructional resources with their own original works in a meaningful way, providing compact educational tools that allow great flexibility in teaching and learning. Material is stored so that it may be retrieved in a nonlinear fashion, depending on the needs or interests of learners. Educators can use multimedia projects to respond spontaneously to students' questions by referring quickly to relevant portions. In addition, students can use multimedia projects to pursue independent study according to their needs or at a pace appropriate to their capabilities. Educators and students want guidance about the application of fair use principles when creating their own multimedia projects to meet specific instructional objectives.

1.3 Applicability of These Guidelines
(Certain basic terms used throughout these guidelines are identified in bold and defined in this section.)

These guidelines apply to the use, without permission, of portions of lawfully acquired copyrighted works in educational multimedia projects which are created by educators or students as part of a systematic learning activity by nonprint educational institutions. Educational multimedia projects created under these guidelines incorporate students' or educators' original material, such as course notes or commentary, together with various copyrighted media formats including but not limited to, motion media, music, text material, graphics, illustrations, photographs and digital software which are combined into an integrated presentation. Educational institutions are defined as nonprofit organizations whose primary focus is supporting research and instructional activities of educators and students for noncommercial purposes.

For the purposes of the guidelines, educators include faculty, teachers, instructors, and others who engage in scholarly, research and instructional activities for educational institutions. The copyrighted works used under these guidelines are lawfully acquired if obtained by the institution or individual through lawful means such as purchase, gift or license agreement but not pirated copies. Educational multimedia projects which incorporate portions of copyrighted works under these guidelines may be used only for educational purposes in systematic learning activities including use in connection with non-commercial curriculum-based learning and teaching activities by educators to students enrolled in courses at nonprofit educational institutions or otherwise permitted under Section 3. While these guidelines refer to the creation and use of educational multimedia projects, readers are advised that in some instances other fair use guidelines such as those for off-air taping may be relevant.

2. PREPARATION OF EDUCATIONAL MULTIMEDIA PROJECTS USING PORTIONS OF COPYRIGHTED WORKS

These uses are subject to the Portion Limitations listed in Section 4. They should include proper attribution and citation as defined in Sections 6.2.

2.1 By students:
Students may incorporate portions of lawfully acquired copyrighted works when producing their own educational multimedia projects for a specific course.

2.2 By Educators for Curriculum-Based Instruction:

Educators may incorporate portions of lawfully acquired copyrighted works when producing their own educational multimedia programs for their own teaching tools in support of curriculum-based instructional activities at educational institutions.

3. PERMITTED USES OF EDUCATIONAL MULTIMEDIA PROGRAMS CREATED UNDER THESE GUIDELINES

Uses of educational multimedia projects created under these guidelines are subject to the Time, Portion, Copying and Distribution Limitations listed in Section 4.

3.1 Student Use:

Students may perform and display their own educational multimedia projects created under Section 2 of these guidelines for educational uses in the course for which they were created and may use them in their own portfolios as examples of their academic work for later personal uses such as job and graduate school interviews.

3.2 Educator Use for Curriculum-Based Instruction:

Educators may perform and display their own educational multimedia projects created under Section 2 for curriculum-based instruction to students in the following situations:

3.2.1 for face-to-face instruction,

3.2.2 assigned to students for directed self-study,

3.2.3 for remote instruction to students enrolled in curriculum-based courses and located at remote sites, provided over the educational institution's secure electronic network in real-time, or for after class review or directed self-study, provided there are technological limitations on access to the network and educational multimedia project (such as a password or PIN) and provided further that the technology prevents the making of copies of copyrighted material.

If the educational institution's network or technology used to access the educational multimedia project created under Section 2 of these guidelines cannot prevent duplication of copyrighted material, students or educators may use the multimedia educational projects over an otherwise secure network for a period of only 15 days after its initial real-time remote use in the course of instruction or 15 days after its assignment for directed self-study. After that period, one of the two use copies of the educational multimedia project may be placed on reserve in a learning resource center, library or similar facility for on-site use by students enrolled in the course. Students shall be advised that they are not permitted to make their own copies of the multimedia project.

3.3 Educator Use for Peer Conferences:

Educators may perform or display their own multimedia projects created under Section 2 of these guidelines in presentations to their peers, for example, at workshops and conferences.

3.4 Educator Use for Professional Portfolio

Educators may retain educational multimedia projects created under Section 2 of these guidelines in their personal portfolios for later personal uses such as tenure review or job interviews.

4. LIMITATIONS—TIME, PORTION, COPYING AND DISTRIBUTION

The preparation of educational multimedia projects incorporating copyrighted works under Section 2, and the use of such projects under Section 3, are subject to the limitations noted below.

4.1 Time Limitations

Educators may use their educational multimedia projects created for educational purposes under Section 2 of these guidelines for teaching courses, for a period of up to two years after the first instructional use with a class. Use beyond that time period, even for educational purposes, requires permission for each copyrighted portion incorporated in the production. Students may use their educational multimedia projects as noted in Section 3.1.

4.2 Portion Limitations

Portion limitations mean the amount of a copyrighted work that can reasonably be used in educational multimedia projects under these guidelines regardless of the original medium from which the copyrighted works are taken. In the aggregate means the total amount of copyrighted material from a single copyrighted work that is permitted to be used in an educational multimedia project without permission under these guidelines. These limits apply cumulatively to each educator's or student's multimedia project(s) for the same academic semester, cycle or term. All students should be instructed about the reasons for copyright protection and the need to follow these guidelines. It is understood, however, that students in kindergarten through grade six may not be able to adhere rigidly to the portion limitations in this section in their independent development of educational multimedia projects. In any event, each such project retained under Sections 3.1 and 4.3 should comply with the portion limitations in this section.

4.2.1 Motion Media

Up to 10% or 3 minutes, whichever is less, in the aggregate of a copyrighted motion media work may be reproduced or otherwise incorporated as part of a multimedia project created under Section 2 of these guidelines.

4.2.2 Text Material

Up to 10% or 1000 words, whichever is less, in the aggregate of a copyrighted work consisting of text material may be reproduced or otherwise incorporated as part of a multimedia project created under Section 2 of these guidelines. An entire poem of less than 250 words may be used, but no more than three poems by one poet, or five poems by different poets from any anthology may be used. For poems of greater length, 250 words may be used but no more than three excerpts by a poet, or five excerpts by different poets from a single anthology may be used.

4.2.3 Music, Lyrics, and Music Video

Up to 10%, but in no event more than 30 seconds, of the music and lyrics from an individual musical work (or in the aggregate of extracts from an individual work), whether the musical work is embodied in copies, or audio or audiovisual works, may be reproduced or otherwise incorporated as a part of a multimedia project created under Section 2. Any alterations to a musical work shall not change the basic melody or the fundamental character of the work.

4.2.4 Illustrations and Photographs

The reproduction or incorporation of photographs and illustrations is more difficult to define with regard to fair use because fair use usually precludes the use of an entire work. Under these guidelines a photograph or illustration may be used in its entirety but no more than 5 images by an artist or photographer may be reproduced or otherwise incorporated as part of an educational multimedia project created under Section 2. When using photographs and illustrations from a published collective work, not more than 10% or 15 images, whichever is less, may be reproduced or otherwise incorporated as part of an educational multimedia project created under Section 2.

4.2.5 Numerical Data Sets

Up to 10% or 2500 fields or cell entries, whichever is less, from a copyrighted database or data table may be reproduced or otherwise incorporated as part of a educational multimedia project created under Section 2 of these guidelines. A field entry is defined as a specific item of information, such as a name or Social Security number, in a record of a database file. A cell entry is defined as the intersection where a row and a column meet on a spreadsheet.

4.3 Copying and Distribution Limitations

Only a limited number of copies, including the original, may be made of an educator's educational multimedia project. For all of the uses permitted by Section 3, there may be no more than two use copies only one of which may be placed on reserve as described in Section 3.2.3. An additional copy may be made for preservation purposes but may only be used or copied to replace a use copy that has been lost, stolen, or damaged. In the case of a jointly created educational multimedia project, each principal creator may retain one copy but only for the purposes described in Sections 3.3 and 3.4 for educators and Section 3.1 for students.

5. EXAMPLES OF WHEN PERMISSION IS REQUIRED

5.1 Using Multimedia Projects for Non-Educational or Commercial Purposes

Educators and students must seek individual permissions (licenses) before using copyrighted works in educational multimedia projects for commercial reproduction and distribution.

5.2 Duplication of Multimedia Projects Beyond Limitations Listed in These Guidelines

Even for educational uses, educators and students must seek individual permissions for all copyrighted works incorporated in their personally created educational multimedia projects before replicating or distributing beyond the limitations listed in Section 4.3.

5.3 Distribution of Multimedia Projects Beyond Limitations Listed in These Guidelines

Educators and students may not use their personally created educational multimedia projects over electronic networks, except for uses as described in Section 3.2.3, without obtaining permissions for all copyrighted works incorporated in the program.

6. IMPORTANT REMINDERS

6.1 Caution in Downloading Material from the Internet

Educators and students are advised to exercise caution in using digital material downloaded from the Internet in producing their own educational multimedia projects, because there is a mix of works protected by copyright and works in the public domain on the network. Access to works on the Internet does not automatically mean that these can be reproduced and reused without permission or royalty payment and, furthermore, some copyrighted works may have been posted to the Internet without authorization of the copyright holder.

6.2 Attribution and Acknowledgement

Educators and students are reminded to credit the sources and display the copyright notice © and copyright ownership information if this is shown in the original source, for all works incorporated as part of the educational multimedia projects prepared by educators and students, including those prepared under fair use. Crediting the source must adequately identify the source of the work, giving a full bibliographic description where available (including author, title, publisher, and place and date of publication). The copyright ownership information includes the copyright notice (©, year of first publication and name of the copyright holder). The credit and copyright notice information may be combined and shown in a separate section of the educational multimedia project (e.g. credit section) except for images incorporated into the project for the uses described in Section 3.2.3. In such cases, the copyright notice and the name of the creator of the image must be incorporated into the image when, and to the extent, such information is reasonably available; credit and copyright notice information is considered "incorporated" if it is attached to the image file and appears on the screen when the image is viewed. In those cases when displaying source credits and copyright ownership information on the screen with the image would be mutually exclusive with an instructional objective (e.g. during examinations in which the source credits and/or copyright information would be relevant to the examination questions), those images may be displayed without such information being simultaneously displayed on the screen. In such cases, this information should be linked to the image in a manner compatible with such instructional objectives.

6.3 Notice of Use Restrictions

Educators and students are advised that they must include on the opening screen of their multimedia program and any accompanying print material a notice that certain materials are included under the fair use exemption of the U.S. Copyright Law and have been prepared according to the multimedia fair use guidelines and are restricted from further use.

6.4 Future Uses Beyond Fair Use

Educators and students are advised to note that if there is a possibility that their own educational multimedia project incorporating copyrighted works under fair use could later result in broader dissemination, whether or not as commercial product, it is strongly recommended that they take steps to obtain permissions during the development process for all copyrighted portions rather than waiting until after completion of the project.

6.5 Integrity of Copyrighted Works: Alterations

Educators and students may make alterations in the portions of the copyrighted works they incorporate as part of an educational multimedia project only if the alterations support specific instructional objectives. Educators and students are advised to note that alterations have been made.

6.6 Reproduction or Decompilation of Copyrighted Computer Programs

Educators and students should be aware that reproduction or decompilation of copyrighted computer programs and portions thereof, for example the transfer of underlying code or control mechanisms, even for educational uses, are outside the scope of these guidelines.

6.7 Licenses and Contracts

Educators and students should determine whether specific copyrighted works, or other data or information are subject to a license or contract. Fair use and these guidelines shall not preempt or supersede licenses and contractual obligations.

APPENDIX A: (as of DECEMBER 12, 1996)
1. ORGANIZATIONS ENDORSING THESE GUIDELINES:
    Agency for Instructional Technology (AIT)
    American Association of Community Colleges (AACC)
    American Society of Journalists and Authors (ASJA)
    American Society of Media Photographers, Inc. (ASMP)
    American Society of Composers, Authors and Publishers (ASCAP)
    Association for Educational Communications and Technology (AECT)
    Association for Information Media and Equipment (AIME)
    Association of American Publishers (AAP)*
    Association of American Colleges and Universities (AAC&U)
    Association of American University Presses, Inc. (AAUP)
    Broadcast Music, Inc. (BMI)
    Consortium of College and University Media Centers (CCUMC)
    Creative Incentive Coalition (CIC)**
    Educational Testing Service (ETS)
    Iowa Association for Communications Technology (IACT)
    Information Industry Association (IIA)
    Instructional Telecommunications Council (ITC)
    Maricopa Community Colleges/Phoenix
    Motion Picture Association of America (MPAA)
    Music Publishers' Association of the United States (MPA)
    National Association of Regional Media Centers (NARMC)

Recording Industry Association of America (RIAA)
Software Publishers Association (SPA)
2. U.S. GOVERNMENT AGENCIES SUPPORTING THESE GUIDELINES:
   U.S. National Endowment for the Arts (NEA)
   U.S. Copyright Office
   U.S. Patent and Trademark Office
3. INDIVIDUAL COMPANIES AND INSTITUTIONS ENDORSING THESE GUIDELINES:
   Houghton-Mifflin
   John Wiley & Sons, Inc.
   McGraw-Hill
   Time Warner, Inc.

NOTES

1. P.L. 105-147 (H.R. 2265), December 16, 1997.
2. *United States v. LaMacchia*, 871 F.Supp. 535 (D. Mass.1994).
3. Criminal Infringement.—Any person who infringes a copyright willfully either—
(1) for purposes of commercial advantage or private financial gain, or
(2) by the reproduction or distribution, including by electronic means, during any 180-day period, of 1 or more copies or phonorecords of 1 or more copyrighted works, which have a total retail value of more than $1,000,
4. P.L. 105-304, signed by President Clinton on October 28, 1998.
5. Intellectual Property Organization (WIPO) Copyright Treaty and the WIPO Performances and Phonograms Treaty.
6. This provision does not take effect for 2 years.
7. U.S.C. § 1201(d) Exemption For Nonprofit Libraries, Archives, and Educational Institutions.
8. See Testimony of Mary Beth Peter, Register of Copyright, before The House Subcommittee on Courts and Intellectual Property on H.R. 2180 AND H.R. 2281, 105th Congress, 1st Session, September 16, 1997.
9. 74 F.3rd 1512.
10. 158 F.3d 674.
11. *West Publishing Co. v. Mead Data Central, Inc.*, 799 F.2d 1219 (1986).